75

HIKES in™

VIRGINIA'S
SHENANDOAH
NATIONAL PARK

HIKES in™

VIRGINIA'S
SHENANDOAH
NATIONAL PARK

SECOND EDITION

Russ Manning

THE
MOUNTAINEERS

Published by
The Mountaineers
1001 SW Klickitat Way, Suite 201
Seattle, WA 98134

First edition (originally published by Mountain Laurel Place as *The Best of Shenandoah National Park: A Guide to Trails and the Skyline Drive*), 1997. Second edition: April 2000.

Published simultaneously in Great Britain by Cordee, 3a DeMontfort Street, Leicester, England, LE1 7HD

Manufactured in the United States of America

Editor: Kris Fulsaas
Project Editor: Christine Ummel Hosler
Maps: Russ Manning, Jerry Painter
All photographs by Russ Manning, unless otherwise noted
Cover and book design by Jennifer La Rock Shontz

Cover photograph: *Fern and pinxter-flower* (Photo by Sondra Jamieson)
Frontispiece: *View from Skyline Drive.*

Library of Congress Cataloging-in-Publication Data
Manning, Russ.
    75 hikes in Virginia's Shenandoah National Park / by Russ Manning. — 2nd ed.
      p. cm.
  Rev. ed. of: The best of Shenandoah National Park / by Russ Manning and Sondra Jamieson. ©1997.
  Includes bibliographical references and index.
  ISBN 0-89886-635-9
  1. Hiking—Virginia—Shenandoah National Park—Guidebooks. 2. Trails—Virginia—Shenandoah National Park—Guidebooks. 3. Shenandoah National Park (Va.)—Guidebooks. I. Title: Seventy-five hikes in Virginia's Shenandoah National Park. II. Manning, Russ. Best of Shenandoah National Park. III. Title.
GV199.42.V82 S484 2000
917.55'90443—dc21
                                              99-050638
                                                  CIP

For Daniel

Shenandoah National Park

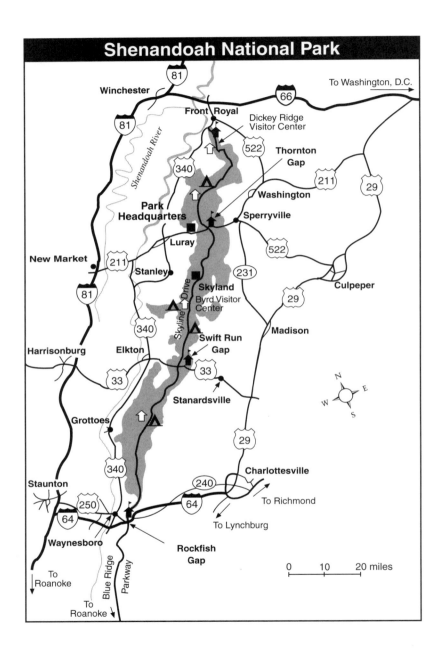

CONTENTS

THE SKYLAND AREA (Map 4)

SKYLAND TO BIG MEADOWS (Map 5)

THE BIG MEADOWS AREA (Map 6)

BIG MEADOWS TO LEWIS MOUNTAIN (Map 7)

LEWIS MOUNTAIN TO SWIFT RUN GAP (Map 8)

SWIFT RUN GAP TO BLACKROCK (Map 9)

BLACKROCK TO ROCKFISH GAP (Map 10)

Key to Map Symbols

——	Interstate/US highways	Ⓢ	Start (Trailhead)
——	State roads	▲	Campground
------	Trail	♠	Entrance station
---AT---	Appalachian Trail	■	Building
——	Stream	⊼	Picnic area
— — —	Park boundary	⇧	Visitor center/Wayside
▬▬▬	Overlook/Parking area	(64)	Interstate highway
•	City/Town	(340)	US highway
▲	Mountain peak	(622)	State highway
⑫	Hike number		

ACKNOWLEDGMENTS

I am grateful to the National Park Service staff at Shenandoah National Park for their support in the preparation of this book. I especially appreciate the support and encouragement of Karen Michaud, chief of interpretation and education, and am grateful for her help in guiding the draft manuscript through the review process.

I thank the NPS staff who reviewed the original manuscript: Reed Engle, cultural resources branch chief; Robbie Brockwehl, concessions specialist; Steve Bair, backcountry wilderness and trails manager; Barb Stewart, park ranger; Rolf Gubler, resource management specialist; Paul Pfenninger, park ranger; Shawn Green, parkwide trail supervisor; and Marsha McCabe, former district interpreter for the South District. Thanks also to former park ranger Janice Pauley, for supplying information on horseback riding. Steve Bair, Rolf Gubler, and Shawn Green provided information for this updated second edition.

I am also grateful to Greta Miller, executive director of the Shenandoah Natural History Association, for meeting with me in the early planning stages.

PREFACE

When I first began an exploration of Shenandoah National Park, I thought that it might not be one of the choice places. It's a linear park, after all, a narrow preserve where, it seemed, you're never really away from it all. It has a road (Skyline Drive) through the middle of it. Nearly all the views from the mountaintops are not of wilderness but of civilization in the surrounding valleys and foothills.

But now I have to say that this is one of my favorite parks. Why? Because of the easy accessibility of the trails from Skyline Drive. Because of the wonderful views of the Shenandoah Valley to the west and, to the east, the Piedmont foothills with their rolling farmlands, rustic inns and bed-and-breakfasts, wineries, and small towns and historic communities. Finally, because of the wilderness of the national park itself—official wilderness, as it turns out, nearly 80,000 acres designated in 1976. But this is also wilderness in actuality: forest that has been reclaimed, cascading streams and falls of water, deep canyons and isolated hollows, and returning wild animals—deer, bear, bobcat, grouse, and more—which I've seen while hiking the trails.

The park contains 520 miles of trails that lead to summits along the Blue Ridge, ranging up to Hawksbill, the highest, at 4,050 feet. You'll wander by falls of water: the tallest, Overall Run, at 93 feet; then upper Whiteoak at 86 feet and South River at 83 feet. But also don't miss the falls of Lewis Spring, Dark Hollow, Rose River, Doyles River, Jones Run, and Cedar Run.

Ultimately, this is a park of views. You'll find seventy-nine named and unnamed overlooks scattered along the length of Skyline Drive and numerous other views of hollows and valleys along the trails—from the summits of Mount Marshall and Pass Mountain in the north; from Stony Man, Hawksbill, and Marys and Bettys Rocks in the central portion; and from Hightop, Blackrock, and Calvary Rocks in the south.

I lead you to all of these places in these hikes that are the best of Shenandoah National Park.

Skyline Drive

Shenandoah Valley as seen from Skyline Drive in the North District

INTRODUCTION

Shenandoah National Park lies along the crest of the Blue Ridge Mountains in northwestern Virginia, occupying about 75 miles of the ridgeline running northeast to southwest. The Blue Ridge is part of the mountainous Appalachian region that stretches from the southern border of New York to central Alabama. To the east of the Blue Ridge stand the foothills of the Piedmont, and to the west lies the Valley and Ridge Province that includes the Shenandoah Valley. The long range of the Blue Ridge Mountains rises 3,000 feet above this surrounding terrain.

When John Lederer, a German explorer, came to the Blue Ridge in 1669, he met the Monacan and Manahoac peoples, whom he found to be peaceful and intelligent, with a symbolic language and a rudimentary calendar. By 1750 the Indians were mostly gone. Many had died of white men's diseases; others were forced off their lands; the remainder were absorbed by other native groups, especially the Iroquois who came to dominate the region.

Other white men had surely penetrated the region earlier than Lederer. But he was the first to leave a written record and so is credited as the first known white man to climb the Blue Ridge in the region of the Shenandoah, an Indian word that likely means "daughter of the stars." This name seems appropriate whether the Indians were taken with the reflection of stars on the waters of the river to the west that now bears the name Shenandoah or they were awed by the upward sweep of mountains that seem to touch the star-studded night.

Fur traders and other explorers followed Lederer into the Blue Ridge. Although a few explorers settled in the wilderness, some with Indian wives, British hold on the region remained tentative. When Alexander Spotswood assumed governorship of the Virginia colony in 1710, he feared the French might push down from the north to claim lands to the west. To check such a movement, he wanted to extend English settlement to the mountains and over the Blue Ridge.

Spotswood encouraged settlement by establishing a fort and trading post near the Blue Ridge and inviting people to settle on land he acquired. Then to open up the mountains themselves, he led an expedition in 1716 to cross the Blue Ridge. Traditionally, it is said that Spotswood's group of fifty, including rangers, Indians, and servants, crossed the mountains at Swift Run Gap, but he may well have crossed elsewhere, probably Milam Gap. The men descended the west side of the mountains and arrived at the South Fork of the Shenandoah River before turning back. Afterward, Spotswood gave each of his explorers a small golden horseshoe and dubbed them the "Knights of the Horseshoe," since the horses had to be shod for the rough mountain journey.

While Spotswood encouraged settlement in the southern Blue Ridge, another Englishman laid claim to the northern mountains. In 1649, King Charles II bestowed on seven English noblemen a region called the "Northern Neck," delineated by Chesapeake Bay, the Potomac River, the Rappahannock River, and a straight line connecting the headwaters of the two rivers. One of the nobles, Lord Culpeper, gained control of the entire Northern Neck, and when he died, the land passed down through his wife and daughter to his grandson, Thomas, the sixth Lord Fairfax.

When Lord Fairfax first visited his property in 1736, he was so enamored of the place that he returned in 1747 to live. Even before his return, Fairfax and the Virginia Colony were disputing the southwestern boundary of the Northern Neck, that straight line running from the source of the Rappahannock to the source of the Potomac. A survey was conducted in 1746 to determine the Fairfax Line. The surveyors chose the headwaters of the Conway River as the source of the Rappahannock, and so surveyed a line from there through Bootens Gap in the Blue Ridge to the Potomac, incorporating 5,280,000 acres in the Fairfax lands. Even so, the line remained in question, and land ownership in this central portion of the Blue Ridge continued to be disputed into the next century, especially with James Barbour, who had purchased much of the southern Blue Ridge in 1730.

Lord Fairfax to the north and Barbour to the south sold and leased Blue Ridge land over time so that the lands were gradually carved into smaller plots as people settled the region. The young George Washington helped survey the Fairfax property.

The lands were first carved into huge plantations. Eventually these were subdivided, becoming smaller farms, but at times still numbering in the thousands of acres. Many of the landowners lived in the valleys to the east and west, using the mountain pastures as summer grazing lands for their livestock. Germans who settled in the surrounding valleys constituted a large percentage of the landowners. English and Scots-Irish constituted most of the remainder, many of whom settled the mountains, living in homes that ranged from clapboard houses to ramshackle cabins. As elsewhere when wilderness was settled, some settlers were squatters who had no documented claim to the land. Others lived on land owned by valley residents with their permission, in exchange for watching over the landowner's livestock and buildings.

Trails and wagon roads crossed the mountains so that valley farmers on the west could trade with populations in the east. The roads crossed the mountain ridge through gaps, such as Thornton, Swift Run, and Rockfish Gaps, which are still in use. Many routes were taken over by individuals and companies who maintained the roadbeds and turned the routes into toll roads. During the Civil War, armies rode through the gaps from battles in the Shenandoah Valley to struggles in the east.

The mountain people cleared the lands for pastures and gardens, using the trees for construction and fuel. They hunted wild animals and gathered nuts, berries, and other forest edibles. What they grew and gathered, they traded for items they could not produce themselves, such as sugar and coffee. Legal (and, after Prohibition, illegal) liquor production was a means for having a cash income. In later years, many mountain people sold their produce to George Pollock's Skyland resort, which operated in the Blue Ridge around the turn of the twentieth century.

Cutting the mountain forests became an industry in which mostly portable sawmills produced lumber and railroad ties. Tanneries in the valley needed tanbark, a source of tannin for making leather from hides; the local people stripped this bark from chestnut oak trees and hauled it off the mountains.

In the western foothills, mining operations pulled iron ore from the earth and used the mountain forests to produce charcoal that fueled the smelting furnaces. Manganese was also mined; when combined with iron, it produced a tough, malleable steel. Copper mines operated on Stony Man Mountain and in Dark Hollow.

A National Park Is Created

In October 1886, sixteen-year-old George Freeman Pollock came to the Blue Ridge Mountains of Virginia to explore his father's land. Pollock's father was one of several principal stockholders in the Miner's Lode Copper Company, which controlled the 5,371-acre Stony Man Mountain Tract. Copper had not been mined there since before the Civil War.

After being shown around the mountain area by a Shenandoah Valley resident, Pollock returned to his father in Washington, D.C., with tales of a high mountain retreat where a refreshingly cool resort could be developed "up among the clouds, sparkling springs, glorious sunsets, majestic views, and only ninety miles from Washington." The senior Pollock soon visited the mountain with other investors. Seeing the quality of the land, the group agreed to back the younger Pollock's dream of a resort on Stony Man Mountain. He led the first camping party in 1888 and sold the first cabin lots at Stony Man Camp in 1889. Through lawsuits, paying off debts, buildings that burned, and the death of his father and another partner in 1893, Pollock gained control of the property and reopened his Stony Man Camp in 1894.

Thus began the decades-long infatuation with the Blue Ridge Mountains of George F. Pollock, or "Polly" as he was known to his friends. Dashing and dauntless, Pollock dressed in hunting shirt and trousers, boots, and ten-gallon hat, with a .45 revolver strapped to his hip and a bugle in hand, which he blew at every opportunity. In such garb, he lavishly entertained his guests.

Most visitors to Stony Man Camp in 1894 stayed in tents furnished with cots, chairs, and washstands, and Pollock advertised "large camp-fires every pleasant night" and "tramping parties . . . every pleasant day." The tents were eventually replaced by wood-frame cottages, shingled in chestnut tree bark or covered in chestnut siding. A recreation hall and a dining hall were constructed. Guests enjoyed picnics, swimming at the head of Whiteoak Canyon, musical shows, and elaborate pageants.

In the forty years that Pollock operated "Skyland," as the Stony Man Camp came to be known, he did much to preserve the mountain region, putting out forest fires and working to prevent logging. Pollock's wife, Addie Nairn, whom he married late in life, purchased the stand of great hemlock trees in the area that came to be called "The Limberlost." So when Secretary of Interior Hubert Work established the Southern Appalachian National Park Committee in 1924 to recommend a location for a national park in the southern Appalachians, Pollock, with Harold Allen and George H. Judd (residents of Washington, D.C., who were frequent visitors to Pollock's Skyland), made an official request that the Blue Ridge be considered for the site of the national park. Ferdinand Zerkel, a local resident of Luray, Virginia, joined with Pollock and the others in promoting the Blue Ridge location.

These supporters of a national park in the Blue Ridge soon formed the Northern Virginia Park Association, with Pollock as president. They convinced members of the National Park Committee to visit the Blue Ridge, and Pollock hosted the members at Skyland, guiding them through the mountains. By the end of 1924, the committee recommended national parks for both the Blue Ridge and the Great Smoky Mountains to the south. For the Blue Ridge park, Harlan P. Kelsey, a member of the committee, suggested the name "Shenandoah," the name of the river and valley to the west.

In 1925, President Calvin Coolidge signed a bill establishing procedures for carving out the two parks. Virginia Governor Harry F. Byrd Sr., who was one of the earliest lot owners at Skyland and supported the formation of a national park, initiated the state's effort to raise funds for purchase of the land. The bill to establish both the Smokies park and Shenandoah National Park was passed by Congress and signed by President Coolidge on May 22, 1926; the initial proposal for Shenandoah was a minimum of 521,000 acres.

Fund-raising by the state was conducted by the Virginia Conservation and Development Commission, headed by William E. Carson, an enthusiastic supporter. A new Shenandoah National Park Association assisted with the effort, with early supporter Ferdinand Zerkel serving as executive secretary. Although fund-raising continued for a few years, there seemed no hope of getting enough money to purchase the required acreage. Thus the minimum was twice reduced, the last time to 160,000 acres.

In 1927, the Potomac Appalachian Trail Club (PATC) formed to promote the route of the Appalachian Trail through the Blue Ridge and to support the establishment of a national park. PATC members built many of the trails now on parklands and still work diligently to maintain them.

Harold Allen, one of the park's early supporters, revived the suggestion of a scenic highway along the spine of the Blue Ridge, which had been proposed as early as 1914. The suggestion was included in the final report of the Southern Appalachian National Park Committee in 1924 as a "skyline drive." In 1930, President Herbert Hoover, who the year before had established his summer White House on the Rapidan River within the proposed boundaries, asked that plans be prepared for a Skyline Drive. Work began in 1931.

In 1933, the Civilian Conservation Corps (CCC) came to fight fires and help develop roads and facilities; there were eventually six CCC camps in the area. In 1934, the central portion of Skyline Drive opened to the public. In 1935, Virginia donated 176,429 acres for the park. President Franklin D. Roosevelt dedicated Shenandoah National Park at Big Meadows on July 3, 1936. A few months later, the northern section of Skyline Drive opened.

In 1934, 465 families (representing 2,276 people) lived within the proposed park boundaries. Only 197 of these families owned the land they lived on; people outside the park owned 93 percent of parklands. During the years the park was established, the numbers fluctuated, with people leaving on their own and others entering the park area. Eventually, the federal government relocated 172 families in new homestead communities surrounding the park, and the state with federal aid took care of 71 families. Most of the mountain homes of these people were torn down. A few elderly folk with their families were allowed to live out their lives at their homes in the park. In 1940, 19 families totaling 78 people still lived in the park; the last resident died in 1979.

Pollock, who had sold his land for the national park, continued to operate the Skyland resort as a concession. In 1937, he sold his business interests in Skyland to the Virginia Sky-Line Company, Inc. Pollock and his wife kept a lifetime lease on their Skyland cottage, called Massanutten Lodge. It still stands, along with several other of the old cottages, among the more modern buildings and cabins that make up the Skyland resort of today.

Other service facilities were constructed at Dickey Ridge, Lewis Mountain, Big Meadows, and Elkwallow by the new concessionaire during 1938–39. In 1939, the southern section of Skyline Drive opened. In 1950, the Shenandoah Natural History Association was established to promote education and interpretation. The Dickey Ridge Visitor Center opened in 1958, and the Harry F. Byrd Sr. Visitor Center opened in 1966. In 1972, ARA Services took over the concessions operation, including Skyland, and is known today as ARAMARK Virginia Sky-Line Company.

In 1976, 79,579 acres of the park were designated wilderness through legislation authored by Virginia Senator Harry F. Byrd Jr. Today, the park encompasses 196,466 acres. Skyline Drive and 365 buildings in the park are included in a Skyline Drive Historic District that was added to the National Register of Historic Places in 1997.

GEOLOGY OF THE BLUE RIDGE

The Blue Ridge Mountains of Virginia are part of the narrow Blue Ridge Province that stretches from New England south into Tennessee and North Carolina, part of the larger Appalachian region. The tallest mountains along the Blue Ridge within the national park are Hawksbill at 4,050 feet and Stony Man at 4,011 feet.

The core rock of the Blue Ridge formed during the early Precambrian period, more than a billion years ago. Deep in the earth, granite (now known as Old Rag granite) and granodiorite (a quartz rock known as the Pedlar Formation) crystallized out of molten rock. In the late Precambrian, more molten rock pushed its way up through fissures so that lava and volcanic ash spread in a thick layer known as the Catoctin Formation over most of what would be the Blue Ridge Mountains. The Catoctin lava covered and intermingled with sediment from highlands to the west; the heat, mineralizing liquids, and gases of the lava solidified the sedimentary material into a layer known as the Swift Run Formation. This mixture of the Catoctin and Swift Run produced rock of three types: greenstones formed from basaltic lavas, purple slate formed from layers of volcanic ash, and sedimentary rock formed from the solidification of sands, clays, and stones.

With the end of volcanism, streams flowed across the lava plains, depositing mud, sand, and quartz stones that later solidified into the Weverton Formation. The land, which began subsiding during the period of volcanism, continued a downwarping, so that bogs and lagoons formed as the eastern sea invaded during the Cambrian period, about 600 million years ago. The sea deposited muddy sands and clays that became the Hampton Formation. Advancing seas left beach sands that later solidified into quartzites of the Erwin Formation.

The Cambrian period was followed by three periods of mountain building due to the tectonic forces of continental plate movement. The earliest uplift occurred during the Ordovician period in mountain building now known as the Taconic orogeny, beginning about 500 million years ago. The uplift was caused by the convergence of an island arc with what would be the North American continent. By the end of the Silurian period, 400 million years ago, the Taconic Mountains had been worn down by erosion.

Then in the Devonian period, new mountains arose in the Acadian orogeny as a result of the collision of the North American plate with northern Europe. Although erosion began to wear down these new mountains, they were not completely eroded before the collision of North America with the African continental plate produced the Alleghenian orogeny, resulting in much folding, warping, and additional uplift 300–250 million years ago. Over the next 100 million years, erosion nearly leveled this range of mountains.

The Appalachian Mountains of today, including the Blue Ridge, are the result of secondary uplift called "isostatic adjustment." In this process, uplift occurs as the weight of overlying layers is removed by erosion and less dense rock below is forced upward by surrounding dense rock. As the ancient mountain range eroded down, reducing the weight above, less dense rock below pushed upward in several intervals of uplift, creating the Blue Ridge anticline, in which stratified layers bent upward. Erosion occurred continuously. Eventually, rock from deep in the earth was uplifted, and erosion exposed the Old Rag granite and the Pedlar Formation that had formed a billion years ago in the Precambrian.

Now, Old Rag granite and Pedlar granodiorite are exposed on some peaks in Shenandoah National Park, especially in the North District. Catoctin greenstone lavas top most of the high ridges, interlayered with Swift Run Formation, especially in the Central District. The Weverton, Hampton, and Erwin Formations are exposed along the slopes of the mountains, in the hollows and creek runs. In the Central and South Districts of the park, magma intruded the Blue Ridge during the Triassic period, leaving vertical dikes of dense, greenish, crystalline rock.

As you explore the trails of Shenandoah, you'll become familiar with these rock types: granite on Old Rag Mountain, Catoctin greenstone along the high ridges, sedimentary rock in the creek hollows.

SHENANDOAH'S FLORA AND FAUNA

At one time or another, large sections of the forests of Shenandoah National Park were cut for lumber, fuel, and tanbark, or just to clear the land for crops and pasture. But small stands of big trees can still be found along some streams in the park, and a few larger patches remain, the most notable being the virgin hemlock forest saved by Addie Pollock.

With the parklands preserved and protected for the last seventy years, the forests have returned. You'll find today rich, dense forests supporting a treasure of plants. These forests consist of 1,200 kinds of vascular plants. Fifty-four of these species are rare or threatened in the state of Virginia or worldwide.

A segregation of forest communities occurs because of differences in elevation, exposure, and moisture.

Chestnut oak forests with associated red oaks, hickories, and pines dominate the exposed ridges and south-facing slopes that are more sunny and dry. The understory consists of dogwood, mountain laurel, and striped maple. Nearly half of the park's land is covered with this chestnut oak forest.

Red oak forests stand farther down the mountain slopes, with white oak, white ash, and red maple associated. Red oaks are probably the most abundant trees in the park.

Cove hardwood forests grow in the moist coves. This type of forest is dominated by red oak, ash, yellow poplar, and basswood. The understory contains spicebush, hop hornbeam, and striped maple.

Yellow poplar forests occur below the cove hardwood forests where streams broaden and the land is even more moist. Among the associated trees are oaks, white ash, white pine, alder, sycamore, and birch. The understory consists of spicebush, maples, and dogwood.

These four are the dominant forests of the park. However, smaller patches of other forests occur. Black locust and oak-pine forests have appeared on lands that were cleared or burned over; the other forest types will eventually replace them. Small hemlock forests can be found along streams. Isolated northern hardwood forests of birch, red oak, and basswood stand on high, rocky, north-facing slopes.

From a distance, a haze can be seen over the mountain forests; it is natural in origin but is today augmented by air pollutants. The trees of the forests expel hydrocarbon molecules of isoprene and more complex terpenes. The molecules break down and recombine, forming molecules large enough to refract sunlight and lend a blue color to the haze. Thus, the mountains have been called the "Blue Ridge."

The forests also support a multitude of wildlife. The most prominent is white-tailed deer. The animal was hunted for its meat, and deer habitat was lost as lands were cleared; so when the park was established, the deer were gone. A few were reintroduced to parklands in 1934, and the numbers have since expanded to several thousand. They can be found along Skyline Drive, grazing on the grass that grows in the open and darting across the road, fearless now that hunting is no longer allowed.

Several hundred black bears inhabit the park, subsisting primarily on nuts, berries, acorns, fruits, insects, and roots. Fewer in number and more shy than deer, bears are more difficult to see. However, spend a week visiting the park and hiking or riding the trails, and you'll likely spot one.

In addition to deer and bears, the park contains another forty-eight species of mammals, including the more familiar squirrel, rabbit, skunk, and opossum and the less familiar bobcat, gray fox, and raccoon. The cougar, or mountain lion, may still roam these mountains; despite several sightings, there is as yet no conclusive proof that these large cats live in the park.

The park streams support twenty fish species, including the brook trout that is native to the Southern Appalachians. Amphibians and reptiles of sixty species lurk on the forest floor. The forest contains about 20,000 insect species. Birds of 200 types either live in the park or pass through with the seasons, including reintroduced peregrine falcons that have successfully reproduced here in the last few years.

Unfortunately, the forests of the Blue Ridge are undergoing change. The gypsy moth was first noticed in the park in 1983; the caterpillars of the moth eat the leaves of oak trees. With repeated defoliation, the oaks become susceptible to diseases and other insects and eventually die. More than 100,000 acres of the park are affected, although at this writing the moths are at a low level.

The hemlock woolly adelgid, another exotic pest, sucks sap from the base of hemlock needles, causing defoliation and eventual death of the tree;

Stand of ferns (Photo by Sondra Jamieson)

most of the park hemlocks are infested. The park staff is spraying an insecticidal soap on some trees at Skyland, Rapidan Camp, Limberlost, and several overlooks in an attempt to save representative stands of hemlock; the soap solution suffocates the adelgids.

With these attacks and the effects from pollutants and other insects, the Blue Ridge forest will change over time. Less susceptible species may come to dominate where the oaks and hemlocks once stood, just as other trees replaced the chestnut tree that was virtually eradicated by a blight in the 1920s and 1930s. The forest will change, but it will endure.

GETTING THERE

Shenandoah National Park lies 70 miles west of Washington, D.C., in north-west Virginia. It's bisected by the 105.4-mile Skyline Drive, which for the most part follows the Blue Ridge crest, with a marker post at each mile, numbered from north to south. Skyline Drive is the primary access for the

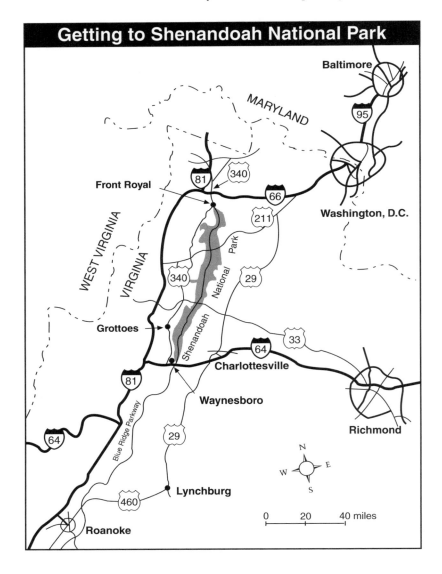

Getting to Shenandoah National Park

park, offering not only scenic overlooks, but also access for most of the trails in the park. US 29 parallels the park on the east, from Charlottesville, Virginia, north to Interstate 66; on the west, I-81 is the major north-south route that parallels the national park. Small airports are located at Charlottesville on the east and Grottoes on the west; Washington, D.C., has the nearest major airports.

At the northern end of Skyline Drive lies Front Royal, just south of I-66. From Washington, D.C., in the east, take I-66 west and at Exit 6 turn south on US 340 to pass through Front Royal and pick up Skyline Drive at the northern end of the park. From I-81 in the west, take I-66 east to Front Royal. From the south, you can enter the park at its southern end at Waynesboro on I-64; that interstate can be taken heading east from I-81 or west from Charlottesville and Richmond, Virginia.

East-west–running highways that pass through major gaps in the Blue Ridge divide the national park into three districts.

US 211, which runs from I-81 on the west to US 29 and I-66 on the east, passes through Thornton Gap in the park. That entrance to the park is 80 miles from Washington, D.C. The North District lies between Front Royal on the park's north boundary and Thornton Gap on US 211.

US 33, which runs from I-81 on the west to US 29 on the east, passes through Swift Run Gap. The park's Central District lies between Thornton Gap to the north on US 211 and Swift Run Gap to the south on US 33.

The South District lies between Swift Run Gap to the north on US 33 and Waynesboro on the park's southern boundary at Rockfish Gap.

For access to Skyline Drive, you must stop at one of the four entrance stations—Front Royal, Thornton Gap, Swift Run Gap, or Rockfish Gap—and purchase either a 7-day or an annual pass.

TRAILS OF SHENANDOAH

More than 500 miles of trails wander through Shenandoah National Park. Most begin at trailheads that are easily accessible from Skyline Drive; a few are reached via side roads entering the park from the east. The trails often lead to summits along the Blue Ridge, offering views of the valleys and foothills below. Others take you past waterfalls up to 90 feet tall. The 75 hikes described in this book are the best of Shenandoah National Park.

Finding Your Way

At virtually every trail junction in the national park, you'll find concrete posts with metal bands imprinted with trail information. If you have a trail map and read the information at each junction, you should be able to find your way around. Still, pay attention to where you are going, so if you lose your way, you can at least retrace your steps to get back to the trailhead. *You must assume full responsibility for knowing where you are going and for not getting lost.*

A trail junction post (Photo by John Amberson, courtesy of Shenandoah National Park)

The park's trails are blazed to help you stay on the path. Hiking trails are marked with a blue blaze; the Appalachian Trail is marked with a white blaze. Horse trails, which may also be used by hikers, have a yellow blaze. A double blaze on any of these pathways indicates a turn in the trail or an intersection.

Always let someone know where you are going. If you get lost, do not leave the trail; search parties will always look for you on the trail first.

You may ride bicycles on Skyline Drive and on public roads in developed areas. Bicycles are not allowed on trails or fire roads, other than the paved path through the Big Meadows complex and the first mile of the Rapidan Fire Road.

Appalachian Trail

For 2,100 miles the Appalachian Trail travels from Mount Katahdin, Maine, to Springer Mountain, Georgia. The AT, as it is commonly referred to, is the longest completed trail in the country and one of the longest in the world. In 1968, it became the first national scenic trail designated in the United States, though the trail itself existed prior to that time.

For 94.5 of those many miles, the AT passes through Shenandoah National Park, for the most part following the crest of the Blue Ridge. The trail enters the park below Compton Gap at the northern end of the park and travels the mountain ridge south, crisscrossing Skyline Drive. When the trail leaves the park near its southern end, just beyond Jarman Gap, it still follows Skyline Drive, crossing it twice more and joining it at Rockfish Gap on the southern boundary of the park to cross over I-64.

Because the AT follows the Blue Ridge crest, it offers some of the best views in the park. In this book, I do not describe the entire AT in the hike descriptions, but I do take you to some of the more interesting viewpoints on the AT, such as Compton Peak, the North and South Marshalls, and Hogback and Pass Mountains in the North District; Marys Rock, The Pinnacle, Stony Man, and Bearfence Mountain in the Central District; and Hightop, Big Flat Mountain, and Blackrock in the South District. Along these sections of the AT, you'll often see "thru-hikers," those headed north to Maine or south to Georgia, or as far as they can walk.

If you intend to hike the AT through the park, you'll need the *Appalachian Trail Guide to Shenandoah National Park,* available through the Potomac Appalachian Trail Club and the Appalachian Trail Conference. You'll find this book for sale at the park headquarters and visitor centers, and from the Shenandoah Natural History Association. Addresses and phone numbers for all of these can be found in the Appendix at the back of the book.

VISITING SHENANDOAH NATIONAL PARK

Your trip to the national park will be safer and more enjoyable if you come well prepared. Even if you are out for only a short time, wear walking shoes or hiking boots. Carry along water, a lunch or snacks, rain gear, and a hat. The Mountaineers recommends that you take the "Ten Essentials" with you on every hike: extra clothing, extra food, sunglasses with UV protection, a knife, a first-aid kit, matches in a waterproof container, some firestarter (candle or chemical fuel), a flashlight, a map, and a compass. A plastic sheet or emergency blanket is also a good idea. Remember to bring sunscreen to prevent sunburn.

If you are camping in the backcountry, you'll need everything for surviving in the open overnight, for however many days you choose to be out. If you are inexperienced, the park rangers or your local outfitters can give advice on the equipment needed.

If you want more detailed information than this book provides on the terrain you are to cover, check the topographical maps that cover the hike you've selected. These maps are available from your local map supplier and at the park visitor centers. At the minimum, bring along a trail map that gives you an overall view of the park and the trail connections; you are given a map of the park when you enter and pay your entrance fee. A much more detailed map for each district of the park is available from the

Potomac Appalachian Trail Club, and a detailed map of the entire park is available from Trails Illustrated. You'll find these for sale at the park headquarters and visitor centers, and from the Shenandoah Natural History Association. Addresses and phone numbers for all of these can be found in the Appendix at the back of the book.

Precautions

Be especially careful when climbing on rocks, hiking along the edge of bluffs, and crossing streams. Do not climb on waterfalls. *You must take responsibility for your own safety, keeping in mind that being in a wilderness or backcountry setting far from medical attention is an inherently hazardous activity.* It is best to travel with someone; if one of you is hurt, the other can care for the injured and go for help.

Severe weather can alter the terrain. A flood in 1995 and a rainstorm in 1996 felled trees and washed out sections of trails. Then an ice storm in 1998 broke tree canopies and brought down more trees, for a time blocking trails and the Skyline Drive. Call the park or stop at a visitor center for current information on the trails.

Many trees in the park have died in the past few years from insect infestation, disease, and cold winters. Be on the watch for falling trees and limbs, and do not set up camp under a dead tree.

The northern copperhead and the timber rattlesnake live in the park; always watch where you put your feet and hands, and give snakes a wide berth. On warm spring and summer days, gnats, black flies, and mosquitoes might be a bother, so carry along insect repellent. Before starting off on a hike, spray your shoetops, socks, and pants with repellent to discourage ticks; one type, the deer tick, can transmit a spirochete that causes Lyme disease. And remember to check yourself after a hike.

Stream crossings can be easy or difficult. After a heavy rain, a stream can be swollen with rushing water. Do not attempt to cross such a stream unless you are sure you can make it. If you cannot see the bottom, you should probably not try to ford.

The weather at Shenandoah is unpredictable, and in spring and fall it can be much colder than you might expect. In cold and wet weather, you face the danger of hypothermia. The symptoms are uncontrolled shivering, slurred speech, memory lapse, stumbling, fumbling hands, and drowsiness. If you are wet and cold, get under some shelter, change into dry clothes, and drink warm fluids. Get in a sleeping bag, if one is available. To prevent hypothermia, stay dry, eat even if you are not hungry, and drink water even when you are not thirsty.

Boil all water in the backcountry at least 1 minute before drinking to destroy bacteria and other microorganisms, including *Giardia lamblia,* a flagellate protozoan causing an intestinal disorder called giardiasis. Filters and water purification tablets can be used, but ask for ones that specifically remove *Giardia*.

If you stay on the trails, you'll probably not come into contact with poison ivy. If you venture off-trail or reach an overgrown section of trail, avoid the three-leaf clusters. You might also encounter stinging nettle, a 1- to 2-foot-high plant with stinging hairs; if you brush against it, you'll feel the stinging for several minutes, but with no lasting effects.

While you're out there, do not pick wildflowers and do not disturb rocks and other natural features, as well as cultural sites. Especially do not collect items found in the wilderness; removal of artifacts prevents accurate archaeological surveys in the future.

Dogs must be kept on a 6-foot leash within the park and on the trails, but are not allowed on the nature trails or the Limberlost, Ridge, Saddle, Dark Hollow Falls, and Bearfence Mountain Trails, due to the difficulty and/or popularity of these trails. To enhance your chances of seeing and not disturbing wildlife, consider leaving pets at home.

Bear Safety

Black bears inhabit the national park. These animals are not extremely dangerous; even so, you should take precautions to not attract or irritate the bears.

A mother bear is very protective of her cubs. If you encounter a mother with cubs, or a cub alone whose mother is surely nearby, back off. Do not advance on the bears and do not place yourself between the mother and her cubs. If you see a bear cub climbing a tree, the mother has probably scooted it up the tree thinking you are a danger; move on.

Black bear (Photo by John Amberson, courtesy of Shenandoah National Park)

If you face a bear, observe from a distance; do not turn and run, which might cause the bear to run after you. If you must back off to avoid an encounter, do so slowly.

Under no circumstances should you feed a bear or leave food for a bear, which could become conditioned to humans and pose a threat to hikers that come after you.

In the backcountry overnight, all food and trash must be hung from a tree to keep it away from bears. Use a long rope over limbs from two trees to suspend your pack a minimum of 10 feet from the ground and 4 feet from any tree or limb. Also to avoid encounters, keep cooking and sleeping areas separate. Keep your tent and sleeping bags free of food odors by not putting food in them. If your pack is free of food odors, you may hang only your food and trash bags, keeping your pack inside the tent with you; also keep your boots in the tent when you retire.

Camping

There are four campgrounds in the national park: Mathews Arm in the North District, Big Meadows and Lewis Mountain in the Central District, and Loft Mountain in the South District. You can make reservations for the Big Meadows Campground by calling the park's camping reservation line (see the Appendix at the back of the book); the others are first-come, first-served. The campgrounds are closed during the winter; check with the park for the dates of operation.

If you're a long-distance hiker on the Appalachian Trail (three or more nights in the park), you can stop overnight at seven huts strung along the AT through the park—Gravel Springs and Pass Mountain in the North District; Rock Spring and Bearfence in the Central District; and Hightop, Pinefield, and Blackrock in the South District—and one outside the park, where the AT is outside the park's southern boundaries, at Calf Mountain.

You may camp anywhere in the backcountry out of sight of roads and other campers, and 30 yards from trails and streams. You must obtain a free backcountry permit, available at the entrance stations, the Dickey Ridge Visitor Center, the Byrd Visitor Center at Big Meadows, the Loft Mountain and Panorama Information Stations, and the park headquarters (located on the west side of the park on US 211), or through the mail from park headquarters.

The park is beginning to create designated campsites at high-use areas, including near the AT huts and along Weakley Hollow Fire Road, which is in the vicinity of Old Rag Mountain in the Central District. Check with the rangers and the visitor centers to find out which areas have designated campsites.

When camping in the backcountry, bury your waste at least 6 inches deep, at least 100 feet away from trails and campsites, and at least 200 feet away from all water sources. Pack out all trash and litter. Campfires are not allowed.

Picnic Areas and Waysides

Each of the seven picnic areas in the park has picnic tables, fireplaces, water fountains, and rest rooms: Dickey Ridge (Mile 4.6), Elkwallow (Mile 24.1), Pinnacles (Mile 36.7), Big Meadows (Mile 51), Lewis Mountain (Mile 57.5), South River (Mile 62.8), and Loft Mountain (Mile 79.5).

The concessionaire for the park, ARAMARK Virginia Sky-Line Company, operates three service areas referred to as "waysides"—Elkwallow in the North District (Mile 24.1), Big Meadows in the Central District (Mile 51), and Loft Mountain in the South District (Mile 79.5). Each wayside offers food, gifts, gasoline, rest rooms, and telephones.

The concessionaire also stocks campstores near the Big Meadows, Lewis Mountain, and Loft Mountain Campgrounds. In addition, there's the Panorama Restaurant and Giftshop in Thornton Gap. These facilities are closed in the off-season; contact the park or the concessionaire for the dates of operation.

Lodging

In the Central District, the park contains two lodges, Skyland and Big Meadows, operated by ARAMARK Virginia Sky-line Company. Both complexes contain lodge rooms, suites, and cabin rooms. ARAMARK also rents cabins and one tent cabin at Lewis Mountain. The lodges are open generally from April to November. Contact ARAMARK for exact dates and advance reservations (see the Appendix at the back of the book).

The Potomac Appalachian Trail Club (PATC) maintains six backcountry cabins: Range View in the North District; Corbin, Rock Spring, Jones Mountain, and Pocosin in the Central District; and Doyles River in the South District. PATC cabins may be rented by the public; call for reservations (see the Appendix at the back of the book). These cabins offer primitive lodging. Bring all supplies with you, including lighting. Bunks, mattresses, blankets, and cooking and eating utensils are supplied. You'll use a woodstove for heating and cooking. You must gather wood, haul water from a spring, and use a privy.

Outside the park, bed-and-breakfasts and inns are available. Check with the local chambers of commerce for further details.

HOW TO USE THIS BOOK

Skyline Drive travels 105.4 miles through the center of the park, following the main Blue Ridge. Each mile is marked by a concrete post on the west side of the road, with mileages running from north to south. The directions in this book indicate the right and left sides of Skyline Drive, based on driving the road from north to south. Right and left are, of course, reversed when driving south to north.

Because Skyline Drive is the main access to trailheads in the national park, I begin by describing hikes at the north entrance, at Front Royal, and work south, ending at Rockfish Gap. For each of the three districts, I include a description of Skyline Drive that tells what you'll encounter as you drive to the trailheads on the road.

The accompanying maps are designed to help you find the access points and trailheads. The hike numbers correspond to the numbers on the maps.

Each hike's summary gives the **distance,** indicating "one-way" whenever the hike is not a loop. I often list the distance to an attraction that is partway along the hike, which can be your destination for a shorter outing.

There is also a **difficulty** rating of easy, moderate, or strenuous. This rating is a subjective judgment of the difficulty of the hike. While a 10-mile hike would be difficult for anyone not used to hiking, it might be rated easy if it has fairly easy walking. So look not only at the degree of difficulty, but also at the distance and the elevation change.

The **elevation gain** or **loss** for a hike indicates a difference in elevation between the hike's highest and lowest points, but there could be several ups and downs along the way. **Elevation change** is given for a loop hike or for a hike that is one-way but the highest or lowest point is along the hike, rather than at the beginning or end.

You'll also find **cautions** about what you might encounter on the hike, such as creek crossings, rocky footing, and steep climbs and descents. Take these into account.

Trail **connections** are included so you can combine several hikes for longer outings.

Following the hike summary, the hike's **attractions** are noted, and directions to the **trailhead** are given. Finally, the hike's **description** details what you'll encounter on the hike. The mileages given are almost always cumulative. If you intend to hike the route in the reverse direction, it will probably be useful to calculate the reverse mileages.

At the back of the book, you'll find selected references, an appendix listing useful addresses and phone numbers, and a standard index.

A Note About Safety

Safety is an important concern in all outdoor activities. No guidebook can alert you to every hazard or anticipate the limitations of every reader. Therefore, the descriptions of roads, trails, routes, and natural features in this book are not representations that a particular place or excursion will be safe for your party. When you follow any of the routes described in this book, you assume responsibility for your own safety. Under normal conditions, such excursions require the usual attention to traffic, road and trail conditions, weather, terrain, the capabilities of your party, and other factors. Keeping informed on current conditions and exercising common sense are the keys to a safe, enjoyable outing.

—The Mountaineers

NORTH DISTRICT

A climb in the ascent of Big Devils Stairs

Parklands in the North District run from Front Royal on the north to Thornton Gap on the south. At the northern end of the district, Dickey Ridge rises to join the main range of the Blue Ridge at Compton Gap. The Appalachian Trail enters the park from the north to also reach Compton Gap and then continue southwest through the park along the crest of the mountains. The significant peaks in this district include Compton Peak, the North and South Marshalls, and Hogback, Neighbor, Knob, and Pass Mountains. At the overlooks along Skyline Drive, you can look west to see the South Fork of the Shenandoah River in Page Valley and Massanutten Mountain in Shenandoah Valley. To the east you can see several of the foothills of the Piedmont. Services here include Dickey Ridge Visitor Center and Picnic Area, Mathews Arm Campground, and the Elkwallow Wayside and Picnic Area. The North District is described in two sections: Front Royal to Keyser Run and Keyser Run to Thornton Gap.

FRONT ROYAL TO KEYSER RUN

This northernmost section of the park, consisting of fewer than 20 miles along Skyline Drive, begins at the Front Royal Entrance Station on Skyline Drive. The name of the community of Front Royal to the north came from an order given by a colonial drill sergeant for his troops to "front the royal oak." Front Royal has lodging and restaurants.

In the park, both the Dickey Ridge Trail and Skyline Drive climb Dickey Ridge to Compton Gap, where the drive turns southwest and the Appalachian Trail picks up, both traveling through the center of the park.

Overlooks offer views to the west of Massanutten Mountain, which divides Shenandoah Valley, with the South Fork of the Shenandoah River in the valley below and the North Fork of the Shenandoah on the far side of Massanutten; the two forks converge north of Front Royal. In 1726, Germans settled Fort Valley, which lies between two ridges of the mountain, and called their community Massanutten, which is likely a German word consisting of *Masse,* meaning "mountain," and *Nute,* meaning "groove" or "furrow," referring to the valley in the mountain. The name was eventually applied to the entire mountain ridge, which is topped with a sandstone that resists erosion and protected the mountain as the surrounding valleys were worn away. Much of Massanutten Mountain is accessible by hiking trails and is part of George Washington National Forest.

Hikes in this section of Shenandoah National Park lead to such attractions as Lands Run Falls, Compton Peak, the North and South Marshalls, and Big Devils Stairs. Short walks lead to the sites of pioneering homesteads that thrived here before the park was established.

Skyline Drive: From Front Royal, as you head up Skyline Drive into Shenandoah National Park, the Dickey Ridge Trail (hike 1) crosses the road at a pullover that provides trail access. You'll then pass a road on the left that leads to residences for the Park Service staff. Stop at the Front Royal Entrance Station at Mile 0.6 to pay your entrance fee.

At Mile 2.0, there's a parking area on the right where, just up the road, the Dickey Ridge Trail crosses. The Shenandoah Valley Overlook at Mile 2.8 offers a view into the Valley and Ridge Province that lies west of the Blue Ridge. Massanutten Mountain rises from Shenandoah Valley, and Front Royal lies to your right.

At Mile 4.6, the Dickey Ridge Visitor Center, where you can get maps and information, stands on the right side of Skyline Drive; the Dickey Ridge Picnic Area is to the south. Across the drive lies the Fox Hollow Nature Trail (hike 2), and the Snead Farm Loop (hike 3) can be accessed from the picnic area.

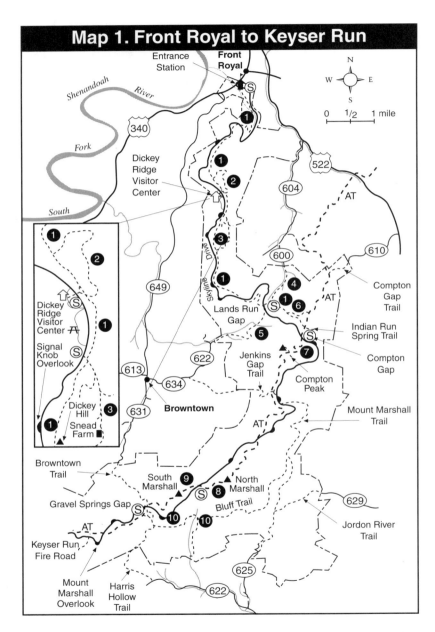

A pullout on the right at Mile 5.3 offers an overlook that has no name but gives a good view of farms in the valley below. This section of valley between the Blue Ridge and Massanutten Mountain to the west is called Page Valley.

From the Signal Knob Overlook at Mile 5.7, you can look across the valley to the two ridges of Massanutten, separated by Fort Valley. The small peak at the northern end of Massanutten became "Signal Knob" when the Confederates during the Civil War used it as a signal location.

At Mile 6.8 lies Gooney Run Overlook, where to the far right you'll see part of Dickey Ridge and a meander of the South Fork of the Shenandoah River in the valley below. The creek in Browntown Valley, Gooney Run, below the overlook of the same name, was named for the dog of Lord Fairfax, the Englishman who inherited this region in the early 1700s.

At Mile 7.3, you can look south from Gooney Manor Overlook to see the North and South Peaks of Mount Marshall and, farther to the left, Compton Peak. "Manor" refers to a parcel of land; Gooney Manor, which included this area, was one of several parcels that Lord Fairfax retained when he sold most of his land.

Pass through Low Gap at Mile 7.9, where the Dickey Ridge Trail (hike 1) crosses; there's a small parking area 100 yards beyond the trail crossing. At Mile 9.2 is Lands Run Gap. Here the Dickey Ridge Trail crosses the drive, and you can access the Hickerson Hollow Trail (hike 4) and Lands Run Gap Road (hike 5).

Skyline Drive reaches Compton Gap at Mile 10.4, where Dickey Ridge joins the main Blue Ridge. The Appalachian Trail (AT) crosses the drive in this gap. Here you can access the Fort Windham Rocks Loop (hike 6) and hike to the summit of Compton Peak (hike 7).

At Mile 10.8, you'll have a view from Indian Run Overlook north across the valley of Indian Run, which has its beginning at Indian Run Spring, and to the east a view out to the Piedmont. Across the drive at this overlook stands an exposed wall of Catoctin lava; toward the north end of the wall, you'll see more examples of columnar jointing (see hike 7).

At Mile 12.35, Skyline Drive dips through Jenkins Gap; a spur road on the west leads a short way to a maintenance area. Just up that road, there's a fire road to the left and, just past that, the Jenkins Gap Trail, which leads west to cross the AT in 150 yards and then descend the mountain and emerge from the park as VA 634 into Browntown.

From the Jenkins Gap Overlook at Mile 12.4, the view is east to the Piedmont with Compton Peak to your left. At Mile 12.5, the Mount Marshall Trail follows an old road into the woods, blocked to vehicle access by boulders. (The trail provides access to the Bluff Trail in 3.5 miles and the Jordon River Trail in 3.9 miles, which heads east to emerge from the park as VA 629. The Mount Marshall Trail then exits the park to become VA 625 at 5.7 miles, which then connects with VA 622.)

At Mile 13.8 you'll reach Hogwallow Flats Overlook, with a wide view to the east of the Piedmont. At Mile 14.2, Skyline Drive passes through Hogwallow Flats, where the AT crosses. Then at Mile 14.9, there's a partial view west from the Browntown Valley Overlook; from the north end you can see Dickey Ridge and the community of Browntown in the valley. You'll also see three hills—Round, Long, and Buck Mountains—that enclose the valley on the west.

At Mile 15.95, parking on the left side of Skyline Drive provides access to the AT for hikes to North Marshall (hike 8) and South Marshall (hike 9). Headed south from Mount Marshall, at Mile 16.1 you can look back over your left shoulder and see the prominent cliffs of North Marshall (it's an easier view if you're driving north).

From the Range View Overlook on the left at Mile 17.1, a sweeping view displays the Blue Ridge range to the south. In the distance, on a clear day, you'll be able to make out the ragged peak of Old Rag Mountain. To the right, look for The Pinnacle and, just to its right, the outcrop of Marys Rock; farther to the right, you may be able to make out the profile of Stony Man.

At Mile 17.6, Skyline Drive reaches Gravel Springs Gap, where the AT crosses the drive. The Browntown–Harris Hollow Road passes through the gap. Here you can access the Bluff Trail for a hike to Big Devils Stairs (hike 10).

From the Gimlet Ridge Overlook at Mile 18.4, the cliffs of South Marshall stand to the far right. Far to the left stands Hogback Mountain, with Gimlet Ridge running out to the right. Toward the end of the ridge, you'll see the three hills that partially close off Browntown Valley below.

At Mile 18.9 the AT crosses Skyline Drive. You can access this AT crossing from Mount Marshall Overlook on the left side of the drive at Mile 19.0. From the overlook, you'll see the two Marshalls to the left and, to their right, the steep slopes of The Peak. Farther to the right, in the valley between the foothills, is the town of Washington, Virginia, sometimes called "Little Washington." A number of the foothills, including The Peak and Wolf, Jenkins, and Keyser Mountains below, were separated from the main Blue Ridge by erosion along a fault line. Keyser Run Fire Road turns off Skyline Drive to the left at Mile 19.4.

1 DICKEY RIDGE TRAIL TO COMPTON GAP

Distance: 9.7 miles one-way
Difficulty: Moderate
Elevation gain: 1,900 feet
Cautions: Steep ascents
Connections: Fox Hollow Nature Trail, Snead Farm Loop, Lands Run Gap Road, Hickerson Hollow Trail, Springhouse Road, AT

Attractions: This is the northernmost hike in this book; it climbs Dickey Ridge, following Skyline Drive to Compton Gap, where Dickey Ridge joins the Blue Ridge. In late summer and early fall, watch for blooming mistflower, clusters of soft blue or blue-violet flowers, and for the oval red berries of spicebush, a shrub more than 3 feet tall. You may notice the nice fruity smell of the bush as you pass, but you'll get more of the pleasant odor by rubbing the leaves together.

Trailhead: The Dickey Ridge Trail begins at the northwest boundary of Shenandoah National Park just south of Front Royal. If you're staying in Front Royal and are close enough to walk to the trail, you'll find it at the end of the sidewalk on the east side of US 340, which passes through town headed south; the sidewalk ends just after the last traffic light, where you'll see the beginning of the trail on the left. If you need to park somewhere, continue south on US 340 and turn left into the national park on the beginning of Skyline Drive. Pass the park entrance sign, and in another 100 yards you'll find a pullover area with a sign that indicates you're headed south on the drive. The Dickey Ridge Trail crosses the drive here, where you may also begin your hike (you'll miss the first 0.2 mile of the trail).

Description: Beginning at Front Royal, bear left off the sidewalk into the woods. At 0.1 mile, the trail passes through an open area grown up in grass. When I hiked the trail, a very long black snake took so much time crossing the path, I finally stepped over it rather than wait any longer; however, stay away from poisonous snakes.

The trail leads back into woods but then at 0.2 mile emerges to cross Skyline Drive at the "Southbound" sign (this is where you begin the hike if you drove in to park your car). Continue straight, back into the woods, which have grown up since the time when these were fields, before the park was established.

At 0.3 mile, the trail parallels a creek on the right, dry most of the year, that's a tributary of the South Fork of the Shenandoah River. You'll see water in the creek at about 0.5 mile. At 0.6 mile there is a side trail to the left (it leads 100 yards up to Skyline Drive, where it emerges above the entrance station); stay straight. After this junction, cross a bridge over the stream you have been following and continue with a slight grade.

Climb more steeply and then follow a low rock wall, which served as a fence, on your left beside the trail. At 1.4 miles, the trail switchbacks right and begins a steeper climb, winding up the slope of Dickey Ridge.

The trail emerges on Skyline Drive at 1.9 miles. To make the crossing, you must walk a few yards up the drive and cross left back into the woods. Still ascending, but not as steeply, you'll pass through a gap in a rock wall at 2.1 miles. At 2.5 miles watch for a path to the right (it leads out to the drive across from Shenandoah Valley Overlook); stay straight.

Continuing up the Dickey Ridge Trail, pass a junction at 4.0 miles with the Fox Hollow Nature Trail (hike 2) to the left; continue straight ahead.

At 4.2 miles, pass a trail on the right (it leads up to the Dickey Ridge

Visitor Center, which lies across Skyline Drive). Just beyond, at another junction where the Fox Hollow Nature Trail crosses again after having looped through Fox Hollow, walk straight through.

You'll see remains of rock fences on your left and at 4.5 miles pass through a gap in a rock fence. The trail reaches a junction at 4.8 miles with the Snead Farm Road (hike 3), which leads down to the Snead Farm; turn left on the road, and then turn off to the right to stay on the Dickey Ridge Trail.

The trail then makes a long ascent to pass just below the summit of Dickey Hill at 5.7 miles; it then descends to a junction with the other end of the Snead Farm Loop to the left at 6.0 miles; keep straight on the Dickey Ridge Trail.

The trail descends to cross Skyline Drive at Low Gap at 7.3 miles. It then ascends to emerge on the drive once again at 8.3 miles. There you'll come out to a parking area, where the Lands Run Gap Road (hike 5) leads to the right; stay straight. Cross the drive and stay right to continue on the Dickey Ridge Trail; you'll also see the Hickerson Hollow Trail (hike 4) beginning on the left.

The Dickey Ridge Trail then ascends Carson Mountain to a junction at 8.9 miles with Springhouse Road on the left; stay straight and connect with the Appalachian Trail at 9.5 miles near Compton Gap; turn right to emerge on Skyline Drive in Compton Gap (Mile 10.4) in another 0.2 mile. (If your goal is to hike the entire length of the park, from here cross Skyline Drive and follow the AT south through the park.)

2 | FOX HOLLOW NATURE TRAIL LOOP

Distance: 1.2 miles
Difficulty: Easy
Elevation change: 250 feet
Cautions: None
Connections: Dickey Ridge Trail

Attractions: The remains of human habitation can still be found in the hollow settled by Thomas and Martha Fox in 1837. The Fox family lived in the hollow until the state of Virginia purchased the land for the park in 1936. The houses and barns are now gone, but signs of past human habitation remain. The trail passes a cemetery where Gertrude and Lemuel Fox are buried. Lemuel, the only son of Thomas and Martha who survived the Civil War, inherited the farm, which later was divided between the four sons of Lemuel and Gertrude.

Trailhead: From the Dickey Ridge Visitor Center at Mile 4.6, take the path that leads straight out from the visitor center and crosses Skyline Drive to the Fox Hollow trailhead.

Description: From the trailhead sign, turn left to hike the loop clockwise. You'll soon connect with the Dickey Ridge Trail (hike 1), which forms this first segment of the loop. Turn left and follow the Dickey Ridge Trail until you reach a junction at 0.2 mile with the Fox Hollow Nature Trail; take it to the right.

The trail begins a descent into Fox Hollow, and at 0.3 mile passes the first of several large rock piles left from the clearing of fields, now regrown in trees. The trail reaches the rock-walled Fox cemetery at 0.4 mile. The trail passes a level area to the left that was the Fox family garden. At 0.5 mile is a concrete box protecting a spring, the first water source for the Dickey Ridge dining hall, which later became the visitor center.

Soon after the spring box, watch for a millstone lying on the ground to the right behind a tree; with no large stream nearby, and so probably no mill, the millstone was most likely brought here for decoration or for use as a stepping stone. The Fox house and barn were located in this area. Just beyond this site, watch for a path on the left to a rock wall that separated the Fox farm from the homesite of Edgar Merchant, their nearest neighbor.

The trail then descends steeply, passing a gathering of golden jewelweed on the left at 0.6 mile. Soon after, watch for a rock-walled depression on the right, and then the trail makes a hairpin turn to the right to follow an old roadbed. On your left, you'll see wire fence topping a row of rock along the roadway. Ascending, the trail curves right at 1.1 miles and reaches a junction with the Dickey Ridge Trail (to the left it leads south to the Snead Farm Road, hike 3, in 0.6 mile); continue straight.

Shortly you'll return to the trailhead and cross back over Skyline Drive to return to the visitor center in 1.2 miles.

3 | SNEAD FARM LOOP

Distance: 2.6 miles
Difficulty: Easy
Elevation change: 500 feet
Cautions: Steep ascent
Connections: Dickey Ridge Trail

Attractions: The Snead Farm site still includes a barn, one of the few remaining structures from the farming communities that existed here before the park was established. The Carter family originally settled the farm; later the Snead family owned it for a few years before it was acquired for the park. In late summer, watch for the yellow blooms of false foxglove and the blue and purple hues of several types of asters.

Trailhead: This loop begins at Mile 5.1 on the east side of Skyline Drive,

Snead Barn

just beyond the exit for the Dickey Ridge Picnic Area, which is next to the visitor center. From the picnic area, you can walk to the trailhead, at the Snead Farm Road, by following the road through the picnic area out to Skyline Drive and then turning to your right; you'll see the Snead Farm Road on the other side of the drive. Or you can park at the Dickey Ridge Visitor Center, then pick up a paved walkway at the far end of the lower parking area and follow it into the picnic area; then follow the preceding directions to the trailhead.

Description: Head down the Snead Farm Road. Soon the Dickey Ridge Trail (hike 1) comes in on the left (it leads 0.6 mile to the Fox Hollow Nature Trail, hike 2); continue straight. Down the Snead Farm Road, in a short distance the Dickey Ridge Trail turns off on the right to continue south; again, stay straight.

At 0.1 mile, the road forks, with the right fork leading up to a communications tower on top of Dickey Hill; stay to the left.

The Snead Farm Road reaches another fork at 0.3 mile (the left fork provides access to the Dickey Ridge water system); take the right fork along the powerline.

At 0.5 mile there's a third fork (the right fork leads up to an instrument tower); stay left.

The Snead Farm lies at 0.7 mile. The house is now gone except for the stone foundations, but the overhanging barn still stands. From the farmsite, the Snead Farm Trail turns to the left at a concrete post. The trail soon curves to the right along an old roadway. At 0.9 mile, begin a steep ascent; the trail winds right and left. At 1.4 miles, the trail reaches a junction with the Dickey Ridge Trail (to the left it continues to Compton Gap); turn right.

The trail passes over Dickey Hill and descends to the Snead Farm Road at 2.6 miles to complete the loop. Turn left to walk back out to Skyline Drive across from the picnic area.

4 | HICKERSON HOLLOW TRAIL

Distance: 1.0 mile one-way
Difficulty: Moderate
Elevation loss: 700 feet
Cautions: Rocky, moderate descent
Connections: Dickey Ridge Trail, Lands Run Gap Road

Attractions: Hickerson Hollow provides a pleasant walk from the crest of Dickey Ridge to the park boundary on the east.

Trailhead: At Mile 9.2, turn into the parking area at Lands Run Gap on the right. (The Lands Run Gap Road, hike 5, leads from here down the mountain; the Dickey Ridge Trail, hike 1, comes down into the parking area and crosses Skyline Drive to the east side.) From the parking area, walk across the road. The Dickey Ridge Trail is to the right; the Hickerson Hollow Trail begins to the left.

Description: Descend from Skyline Drive on an old roadway. Soon, the Hickerson Hollow Trail begins to wind down the mountain, following a tributary of Happy Creek; this stream joins the main creek outside the park in Harmony Hollow. At 0.3 mile, pass through a wet area with trickles of water running across the trail and under the old roadbed in culverts.

At 0.7 mile, a stream on the right crosses under the road to join the main tributary on the left. Its collection of waters now shows small pools and cascades; the stream is open to catch-and-release fishing only. At 0.9 mile, cross a footbridge over another stream that comes in from the right; horses must ford. Then at 1.0 mile is the park boundary, where the road is blocked to vehicle access by slabs of rock.

(The road continues outside the park as VA 600. You can access the trail at this end by going east out of Front Royal on US 522, turning right, south, on VA 604, and continuing to a left turn to the park boundary. Entering the park here, you can hike the Hickerson Hollow Trail in reverse, up to Skyline Drive, and then connect with the Dickey Ridge Trail or cross the drive to descend the mountain on the other side down Lands Run Gap Road.)

5 | LANDS RUN GAP ROAD

**Distance: 2.0 miles one-way; Lands Run Falls,
    0.6 mile one-way**
Difficulty: Easy
Elevation loss: 900 feet
Cautions: Rocky, moderate descent
Connections: Dickey Ridge Trail, Hickerson Hollow Trail

Attractions: This old road gives short access to a cascading waterfall on Lands Run, which is open to catch-and-release fishing only. In the narrow falls, the water jumps from ledge to ledge as it drops steeply into Browntown Valley.

Trailhead: Begin at the parking area on the right at Mile 9.2 on Skyline Drive, in Lands Run Gap. (The Dickey Ridge Trail, hike 1, crosses the drive here, and the Hickerson Hollow Trail, hike 4, is on the east side of the drive).

Description: At the far end of the parking area, the Lands Run Gap Road descends the mountain. Go around the chain that blocks vehicle access, and proceed down the road. As the road zigzags right and left, it begins descending more steeply.

At 0.6 mile the road passes over Lands Run, which flows under the road in a culvert. A path to the right leads to the top of Lands Run Falls.

Take care exploring at the edge; the rocks can be slippery.

The road continues to wind down the mountainside, crossing a tributary of Lands Run and emerging at the park boundary at 2.0 miles. (The road then joins VA 622 outside the park, which can be accessed from Browntown, on VA 649, via VA 634.)

6 | FORT WINDHAM ROCKS LOOP

Distance: 2.0 miles
Difficulty: Easy
Elevation change: 100 feet
Cautions: None
Connections: Dickey Ridge Trail, AT

Attractions: A pleasant hike through the woods, this loop takes you by the outcrop of Fort Windham Rocks—not spectacular as outcrops go, but a good example of Catoctin lava formations; rocks exposed in the surrounding terrain are Pedlar granodiorite. In early fall watch for the red berries of spicebush and, low to the ground, the spike of red berries of jack-in-the-pulpit.

Trailhead: On Skyline Drive at Mile 10.4, in Compton Gap, trailhead parking lies on the left.

Description: Head up the old road at the far end of the parking area. This is the Appalachian Trail (AT), which crosses Skyline Drive here to continue south.

With a gentle ascent, you'll reach a four-way junction at 0.2 mile on Carson Mountain. (To the right, a trail descends to Indian Run Spring in 0.2 mile and a Potomac Appalachian Trail Club maintenance building; straight ahead, the AT continues north.) Turn left on the Dickey Ridge Trail, which begins here at the junction with the AT.

At 0.4 mile, you'll reach the Fort Windham Rocks outcrop. Continue straight on the Dickey Ridge Trail to a junction at 0.8 mile with Springhouse Road. (To the left the road has been abandoned; straight ahead the Dickey Ridge Trail, hike 1, descends Dickey Ridge to Front Royal in 8.9 miles—the section from here to Lands Run Gap is open to horses, to allow access to Lands Run Gap Road and the Hickerson Hollow Trail from Springhouse Road, which is also a horse trail.) Turn right on Springhouse Road.

The last time I walked here, a dead tree fell just after I passed; take heed of the warnings to watch for falling trees. The road curves right, passes an abandoned road to the left, and reaches a junction at 1.5 miles with the AT.

(To the left, the AT heads north 1.1 miles to a junction with the Compton Gap Trail, which leads out to VA 610 in another 0.5 mile—the Compton Gap Trail and this section of the AT are a horse route that ties in with Springhouse Road; from the junction with the Compton Gap Trail, the AT emerges from the park to continue down the mountain, passing the Tom Floyd camping area, and finally reaching US 522 in 5.6 miles.) Turn right on the AT to complete this loop.

At 1.8 miles you'll return to the four-way junction (the Indian Run Spring Trail is to the left and the Dickey Ridge Trail is to the right); stay straight to return to the parking area at Compton Gap at 2.0 miles.

7 | COMPTON PEAK

Distance: 1.0 mile one-way; 0.4-mile side trip
Difficulty: Moderate
Elevation gain: 500 feet
Cautions: Rocky, steep descent on side trip
Connections: AT

Attractions: This short hike on the Appalachian Trail (AT) takes you to the summit of Compton Peak, where a couple of overlooks offer views of the surrounding mountains and examples of rock fractures called columnar jointing. The once-molten Catoctin lava, when cooled, fractured along crystalline lines, creating polygonal structures of four, five, and six sides.

Trailhead: At Mile 10.4, the AT crosses Skyline Drive in Compton Gap. From the parking area on the left, which also provides access to Fort Windham Rocks (hike 6), walk across the drive and to your left to pick up the AT.

Description: Follow the AT up the slope into the woods. In 50 yards, the trail turns left to head south. Ascending Compton Peak, you pass a large block of stone on the left at 0.2 mile, and then the trail swings right. Another block of stone on the trail presents an example of columnar jointing. You'll see more of this later on.

At 0.5 mile, the trail swings left in the ascent. There's another block of stone on the left, and then the trail swings right. At 0.8 mile, the AT reaches a four-way junction near the top of Compton Peak. (The AT continues straight, headed south toward Jenkins Gap; the trails right and left lead to viewpoints.) Take the left trail first (a 0.4-mile side trip).

Descend to a ledge in 0.1 mile, where the trail bears left and drops down the rock. You'll then walk up to a rock outcrop at 0.2 mile, where you can scramble up for a partial view to the south. But more interestingly,

the rock you're standing on is another example of Catoctin lava columnar jointing. Unfortunately, the columnar structure is not apparent on
top because of erosion. To the right of the rock, you can scramble down
the steep chute between two blocks of stone to get to the bottom, where
you'll see the four-, five-, and six-sided columns protruding from the
rock. Only agile hikers should attempt this scramble down to the bottom. Return to the four-way junction, having hiked a total of 0.4 mile on
this side trip.

Back at the four-way junction, now take the right path, which takes you
over the summit of Compton Peak at 0.9 mile (1.3 miles including the side
trip) and then down to a bare rock ledge at 1.0 mile (1.4 miles with the
side trip) that offers a view to the north. You're facing Dickey Ridge as it
ascends to meet the Blue Ridge.

8 | NORTH MARSHALL

Distance: 0.6 miles one-way
Difficulty: Moderate
Elevation gain: 270 feet
Cautions: Rocky, drop-offs
Connections: AT

Attractions: The North and South Marshalls were once part of the Manor
of Leeds, one of the parcels of land retained by Lord Fairfax. When he died
in 1781, his lands were sold to a group of investors, one of whom was John
Marshall, who obtained the Manor of Leeds. Marshall's father, Thomas,
had been a surveyor of Fairfax lands with George Washington and had
given the name Marshall to the mountains. You'll have grand views from
rock outcrops near the north summit of Mount Marshall.

Trailhead: Where the Appalachian Trail (AT) crosses Skyline Drive at
Mile 15.95, turn into the parking area on the left. The AT passes the back
end of the parking area (to the right, it leads to South Marshall, hike 9);
take the AT to the left, heading north.

Description: Begin ascending the slope of North Marshall. The trail
swings right and then left; through the trees in winter you'll see rock bluffs
ahead. At 0.2 mile, the trail switchbacks right in a steeper ascent and, soon
after, reaches the rock bluff you saw from below; here the trail switchbacks left.

Then ascend to a rock outcrop on the left at 0.3 mile that affords an
expansive view west, with South Marshall and Hogback Mountain to the
left, Browntown Valley below, and Dickey Ridge to the right; Hogback

Mountain has the radio towers. The trail turns right at this viewpoint and then turns left to continue to ascend the rocky slope of the mountain. At 0.4 mile, you reach the ridgeline at another rock outcrop on the left that offers a similar view. The trail levels out along the ridge, passing a couple more outcrops, then making one more ascent to reach the summit of North Marshall at 0.6 mile. The rock outcrops there do not offer a view. (From the summit, the AT descends the rocky slope to eventually cross Skyline Drive in Hogwallow Flats in another 1.5 miles.)

9 | SOUTH MARSHALL

Distance: 0.9 mile one-way
Difficulty: Moderate
Elevation gain: 210 feet
Cautions: Rocky
Connections: AT

Attractions: The North and South Marshalls were once partly owned by John Marshall, who served as Chief Justice of the U.S. Supreme Court 1801–1835. Mount Marshall is named for his father, Thomas. Rock outcrops near the summit of South Marshall offer views to the west. In early spring, the tops of the bare trees are brushed with a maroon color as new growth pushes upward in the warming sun; despite snow still on the ground and the gray of rock and tree, leaves and flowers will soon color the path.

Trailhead: Where the Appalachian Trail (AT) crosses Skyline Drive at Mile 15.95, turn into the parking area on the left. The AT passes the back end of the parking area (to the left, it leads to North Marshall, hike 8); take the AT to the right, heading south.

Description: At 0.1 mile, the trail crosses Skyline Drive at an angle to the east side and then ascends gradually through the woods, passing mounds of exposed rock.

The trail levels off at 0.4 mile on the shoulder of South Marshall, and then ascends once more to the summit at 0.6 mile. There are no views there; but continue across the summit and begin descending the other side until, at 0.7 mile, a side path leads to the right to a rock outcrop and a view west. Continue on down the trail through a snaking curve to a path to the right and another outcrop at 0.9 mile, with a 180-degree view west. Hogback Mountain with its radio towers stands to the left. (From the overlook, the AT continues across the slope of South Marshall to emerge at Gravel Springs Gap and cross Skyline Drive in another mile.)

10 | BIG DEVILS STAIRS

**Distance: 3.4 miles one-way; Big Devils Stairs
Overlook, 2.4 miles one-way**
Difficulty: Moderate (strenuous if you return up the
creekbed)
Elevation loss: 1,400 feet
Cautions: Steep descent, exposed bluffs
Connections: Browntown Trail, AT, Bluff Trail, Harris Hollow
Trail

Attractions: This trail provides a view of one of the deep canyons of the park. Water murmurs in the depths of the narrow gorge. Circling ravens give mournful calls that echo off the massive rock walls. If you're an experienced hiker, you can return up the creekbed during the dry seasons for a little adventure. In early fall, I circled pools and spillways fairly easily. But at two locations, I encountered rock walls that had to be climbed to the levels above in order to continue up the streambed; the ascents do not require rock climbing expertise, but you must be agile.

Trailhead: At Mile 17.6, pull into the parking area on the left at Gravel Springs Gap. The old road here was once the Browntown–Harris Hollow Road, which crossed the mountain. (On the right side of Skyline Drive, this old road is now the Browntown Trail, which descends the mountain to emerge from the park and connect with VA 631; the access there is not readily visible.) The Appalachian Trail (AT) from the north joins this road just off Skyline Drive, then crosses the drive to head south on the left side of Skyline Drive. From the parking area, take the AT into the woods, headed south; the trail parallels the old road as it leads down to the Gravel Springs Hut.

Description: Along the AT in 0.1 mile, there's a junction (the AT continues straight); turn left onto the Bluff Trail to descend to another junction, at 0.3 mile, with the old road you've been paralleling. (To the right lies the Gravel Springs Hut, where long-distance hikers may camp—the spring is at the junction with the road; straight ahead, the old Browntown–Harris Hollow Road goes on down the mountain but has become overgrown beyond the hut.) Turn left on the road, and then turn right to continue on the Bluff Trail.

At 0.4 mile is another junction (the Harris Hollow Trail to the left leads up the old road for access back to Skyline Drive); stay straight and curve right for the short distance that the Harris Hollow Trail and the Bluff Trail coincide.

At 0.5 mile is yet another junction (the Harris Hollow Trail continues straight to rejoin the old roadway headed east down the mountain, where it emerges from the park on VA 622); stay left on the Bluff Trail.

Pass along the slope of South Marshall. The trail passes through rock outcrops and crosses small flows of water. At 1.0 mile, pass through an open area with displays of blue asters in late summer and early fall. The trail drops off to the right and then ascends back to the level at 1.6 miles.

At 1.7 miles, step over a crevice with a stream that is the head of Big Devils Stairs, and continue on to a junction at 1.8 miles (the Bluff Trail continues on across the flank of North Marshall to connect with the Mount Marshall Trail in another 2.1 miles); turn right on the Big Devils Stairs Trail.

The trail winds down the mountain through stands of laurel out to a bare rock view on the east edge of the canyon at 2.4 miles. The trail skirts the edge of the canyon and then turns away from the edge into the woods, steeply descending the rocky slope by switchbacks to the mouth of the canyon at 3.4 miles. Rockhop the stream, which is a tributary of the Rush River; on the other side, the trail continues downstream a few paces to the park boundary and private land, which you may not cross; from here, return up the mountain the way you came along the Big Devils Stairs Trail.

(If it is the dry season and the water in the stream is low, you may follow the streambed back up the canyon. This alternative route is only for experienced hikers and explorers; do not attempt this return up the canyon if you do not have experience in off-trail hiking. Also be aware that you may run into stinging nettle, a plant that will sting your bare skin. Eventually you'll emerge at the head of the canyon to reconnect with the Bluff Trail. Then turn left on the Bluff Trail to retrace your steps back to Gravel Springs Gap.)

KEYSER RUN TO THORNTON GAP

In this lower section of the North District, the park boundaries broaden, providing opportunities for longer hikes. Trails lead to Little Devils Stairs, Overall Run Falls, Knob Mountain, Byrds Nest No. 4 Shelter, and Pass Mountain.

The North District ends at Thornton Gap, where US 211 passes over the Blue Ridge Mountains. Thornton Gap bears the name of Francis Thornton, who owned much land, a mansion, and a mill to the east in the early 1700s. The road through Thornton Gap was built in 1746, one of the first roads to cross the Blue Ridge. Andrew Russell Barbee later operated it as a toll road and took in lodgers at his home, Hawsburg, located in the gap.

You can enter or exit the park at the Thornton Gap Entrance Station. To the west on US 211, you can descend into Luray for restaurants and inns. On the east side of the park, US 211 heads to additional services in Sperryville. Skyline Drive continues through Thornton Gap on into the Central District.

Skyline Drive: At Keyser Run Fire Road at Mile 19.4, a walk down the road provides access to the Pole Bridge Link Trail (hike 11) and the Little Devils Stairs Trail (hike 12). Continuing on the Skyline Drive from Keyser Run Fire Road, at the Little Hogback Overlook at Mile 19.7, you'll have a view down Browntown Valley with Hogback Mountain to your left. The Appalachian Trail (AT) can be accessed by a short path at the north end of the overlook parking; north on the AT for 0.1 mile offers a view west from the summit of Little Hogback.

At the Little Devils Stairs Overlook at Mile 20.1, you'll see the gorge of Little Devils Stairs below and "Little" Washington in the distance. At Mile 20.4, a graveled pullout on the right provides access to the AT in a 400-yard uphill hike to a hang glider launch site. At Mile 20.8, the AT crosses Skyline Drive; you'll also see a service road on the right for the radio towers on the summit of Hogback Mountain. Just beyond this AT crossing lies the Hogback Overlook; the ridge running down from Hogback Mountain splits into Mathews Arm to the left and Gimlet Ridge to the right.

At Mile 21.1, a paved parking area on the right provides access to the AT, which leads to the Overall Run Trail (hike 13). From Rattlesnake Point Overlook at Mile 21.9 on the left, you'll have a bird's-eye view of Pignut Mountain, straight out from the overlook. The rock exposed on the other side of the drive is a good example of Catoctin basalt. The AT crosses the drive just to the south of the overlook; north along the AT it's 0.6 mile to the Tuscarora/Overall Run Trail (hike 13).

Map 2. Keyser Run to Thornton Gap

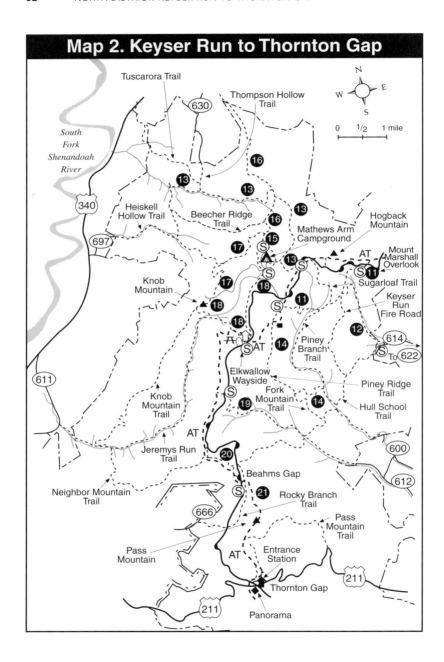

At Mile 22.1, a road on the left turns up to the Piney River Maintenance Area, where you can access the AT and the Piney Ridge Trail (hike 14). At Mile 22.2 is a road to the right that leads to the Mathews Arm Campground, where several trails are accessed, including the Traces Nature Trail (hike 15), the Mathews Arm Trail (hike 16), and the Weddlewood and Heiskell Hollow Trails (hike 17).

The AT crosses the drive just before the Elkwallow Wayside at Mile 24.0, where you can get gas and food. Just beyond, at Mile 24.1, the Elkwallow Picnic Area lies on the right. The Jeremys Run Trail (hike 18) begins at the back of the picnic area.

At Mile 24.2, you'll pass the one-way road emerging from the Elkwallow Picnic Area. Then at Mile 25.4, parking on the left provides access to the Thornton River Trail (hike 19).

From Jeremys Run Overlook at Mile 26.4, you'll have a view of the valley of Jeremys Run bordered by Neighbor Mountain on the left and Knob Mountain on the right. At Mile 26.8, paved parking on the right provides access to connecting trails to the Neighbor Mountain Trail and the Appalachian Trail.

The Thornton Hollow Overlook at Mile 27.6 offers a view to the east; on the far left you'll see Piney Ridge running down into Thornton Hollow below; Pignut Mountain stands behind the ridge. The mountain in midview is Fork Mountain, to the right but more distant is Oventop, and farther to the right stands Pass Mountain.

At Mile 28.2, there's paved parking on the left for the Hull School Trail, which descends northeast, intersecting with the Thornton River, Fork Mountain, and Piney Branch Trails, and beyond, connecting with the Keyser Run Fire Road. Across the drive from the Hull School Trail, a service road that is also the Neighbor Mountain Trail heads up the mountain to the Byrds Nest No. 4 day-use shelter. Skyline Drive reaches Beahms Gap at Mile 28.5, where you can take a loop hike to Byrds Nest No. 4 (hike 20). Here you can also access the AT for a hike to a view from Pass Mountain (hike 21).

At Mile 30.1 on Skyline Drive, you'll reach the Pass Mountain Overlook, which offers a view down Kemp Hollow with Neighbor Mountain to the right. You'll see Massanutten in the distance, marked with the notch of New Market Gap; US 211 runs from the gap across the valley to Luray below. From the overlook, a 0.2-mile loop trail begins straight out and circles left to return through a gap in the fence to the left.

Continuing on Skyline Drive, you'll pass the service road for the Pass Mountain Hut on the left at Mile 31.4 just as you enter Thornton Gap; the AT follows this service road down into Thornton Gap to cross the drive, descend to cross US 211, and pass below the Panorama complex.

As you drive into Thornton Gap, notice Marys Rock at the peak of the mountain on the other side. US 211 divides the North District of the park from the Central District as you pass through the gap. On the left stands the Thornton Gap Entrance Station.

11 KEYSER RUN FIRE ROAD, POLE BRIDGE LINK TRAIL, PINEY BRANCH TRAIL, AND AT

Distance: 6.8-mile loop
Difficulty: Moderate
Elevation change: 800 feet
Cautions: Skyline Drive crossings, steep ascents, creek ford
Connections: Little Devils Stairs Trail, Sugarloaf Trail

Attractions: A quiet walk through backcountry and views along the Appalachian Trail (AT) to the west make this a good loop hike. Near the end of the hike, there's a side path to a hang glider launch site, where the view is straight down Browntown Valley to Dickey Ridge. Just beyond the launch site, there's another view to the left under a powerline that runs to the radio towers on the summit of Hogback Mountain.

Trailhead: At Mile 19.4, turn on the Keyser Run Fire Road on the left, where you'll find a paved parking area. On the other side of the drive, a short connecting trail leads to the AT; this is the return route.

Description: To walk this loop clockwise, head down the Keyser Run Fire Road past the chain gate. The road descends gently, crosses a small tributary of Keyser Run at 0.5 mile, and reaches an intersection at 1.0 mile at a point called "Fourway." (To the left the Little Devils Stairs Trail, hike 12, descends through a narrow, steep canyon; straight ahead, the Keyser Run Fire Road continues down the mountain to cross the Park Boundary in another 3.3 miles.) For this hike, continue just a few paces down the road from the Little Devils Stairs turnoff and turn right on the Pole Bridge Link Trail.

The trail follows an old roadway through the woods. A couple of small wet-weather streams cross the trail. At 1.6 miles, there's a junction (the Sugarloaf Trail to the right joins the AT in 1.4 miles—where you can head north back to Keyser Run Fire Road for a shorter loop of 4.7 miles); stay straight on the Pole Bridge Link Trail to make the longer loop.

The trail descends gently, eventually winding down and ending at a junction at 2.0 miles with the Piney Branch Trail. (To the left, the Piney Branch Trail heads down the mountain to the east to follow the Piney River, cross the Hull School Trail, and emerge from the park in 4.4 miles as VA 600.) Stay straight, now on the Piney Branch Trail heading west.

Soon two streams that are tributaries of the Piney River cross under the trail in culverts, and at 2.1 miles you must ford the main branch of the Piney River. Here is where a pole bridge once stood, from which the Pole Bridge Link Trail got its name. The bridge washed away some time ago.

From the ford, continue up the old roadway, which ascends an eroded, rocky section and then ascends more steeply as the road curves right. At 2.8 miles the trail crosses water from a spring on the left. The old roadway curves right two more times as it ascends the ridge to reach a junction with the Appalachian Trail at 3.4 miles. You'll emerge in a clearing where the service road from the Piney River Maintenance Area descends to the Range View Cabin. (The AT to the left follows the road south for a few paces and then turns left off the road to pass near the cabin in 0.4 mile.) Turn right to walk the AT to the north on a wide path.

Begin ascending and curve left to walk through boulders, then descend to a crossing of Skyline Drive at 3.8 miles. Just to the right on the drive, you'll see the Rattlesnake Point Overlook.

Back among trees and boulders, make a steep, winding ascent of Hogback Mountain. At 4.0 miles the trail tops the first of four peaks of Hogback at a rock outcrop. Then descend, swinging left around another mound of rocks, and begin a long, steep ascent of the second peak. At 4.4 miles, the trail reaches a junction (the Tuscarora/Overall Run Trail, hike 13, goes to the left, with the Big Falls of Overall Run 2.8 miles down that trail); stay straight on the AT.

Continue to ascend, and top the second peak of Hogback Mountain at 4.5 miles. Then descend to pass by AT-access parking and cross Skyline Drive at 4.8 miles. Ascend once again to top the third peak of Hogback at 4.9 miles. The trail then descends, passing above the Hogback Overlook on Skyline Drive and swinging right to a junction (the Sugarloaf Trail to the right leads 1.4 miles down to the Pole Bridge Link Trail); stay straight here.

Swing left up steps and cross Skyline Drive at 5.1 miles. On the other side of the drive, walk up the service road that leads to radio towers. Soon the AT turns off to the right. Just after the turn, you'll see an old path on the right that leads out to the drive, but stay straight to ascend steeply, cross the service drive, and reach the fourth summit of Hogback Mountain at 5.3 miles, where you'll be among radio towers and small service buildings. Across the summit, begin a descent of Hogback Mountain.

Soon, a path on the left leads to the edge of the mountain and a hang glider launch area. Continuing down the AT, you reach a junction at 5.4 miles (a side path to the right leads down to Skyline Drive in 400 yards; there's a little parking there if you want to make a short trip to the hang glider launch site); the AT continues straight.

Cross a couple of knolls and then begin a steep descent. With several switchbacks, you'll drop below the level of Skyline Drive into the gap between Hogback Mountain and Little Hogback. Pass below Little Hogback Overlook and ascend to a junction at 6.3 miles (a path to the right leads from the AT to the overlook); stay straight on the AT.

Continue ascending to bear left over the low summit of Little Hogback to where the AT turns right at 6.4 miles. At this turn, a path leads left out to a rock outcrop and a good view of Hogback Mountain to your left, with Gimlet Ridge running down to Browntown Valley. Continue on the AT, which descends to a junction at 6.7 miles (the AT continues straight toward Gravel Springs Gap); turn right onto the access path to Keyser Run. Cross Skyline Drive at 6.8 miles and close the loop at the Keyser Run Fire Road parking area.

12 LITTLE DEVILS STAIRS TRAIL AND KEYSER RUN FIRE ROAD

Distance: 5.5-mile loop
Difficulty: Strenuous
Elevation change: 1,400 feet
Cautions: Steep rocky ascent, creek crossings
Connections: Pole Bridge Link Trail, Hull School Trail

Attractions: This ascent through a narrow canyon is one of the most interesting hikes in the park. In spring, petals from yellow poplar blooms litter the path; this tall tree with large, showy flowers is actually a member of the magnolia family. Watch for stands of maidenhair fern in spring, and in summer, blackberries and raspberries. For a change of pace, this hike begins outside the park, near "Little" Washington, a picturesque hamlet known for its inns and bed-and-breakfasts.

Trailhead: On US 211/522 south of Washington, Virginia, turn west on VA 622. At 2.0 miles, turn left on VA 614, which becomes a graveled road. At 5.2 miles, trailhead parking is on the right. Entering the park here, you'll pay an access fee, unless you already have the Skyline Drive park pass. (You can also access this loop hike along the Keyser Run Fire Road from Skyline Drive at Mile 19.4; if so, join the hike description midway at the four-way junction.)

Description: The trail enters the woods and drops to cross a small creek, then a larger creek. Bear to the right past piles of stone from once-cleared fields. At 0.1 mile, curve left up the cove of Keyser Run, the stream flowing from Little Devils Stairs canyon.

Stone walls and piles of stone remain from the time before there was a national park. Drop through a drainage area and ascend to Keyser Run,

Falls in Little Devils Stairs

crossing the creek at 0.8 mile. Then make a steep, rocky ascent upstream, crossing the shallow creek several times. At 0.9 mile, watch for a huge poplar on the right.

The trail continues up the cascading creek, crossing a talus slope, and at 1.2 miles it enters Little Devils Stairs, a narrow, vertical-walled canyon. Keep an eye on the blazes through the rocky gorge. At 1.5 miles, the creek glides down smooth rock; soon after, you'll pass through a rock chute just after a cascade.

At 1.7 miles, the trail turns left away from the creek just before a cascading falls. It then winds up the slope to reach the Fourway junction with the Keyser Run Fire Road at 2.0 miles. (To the right, the fire road reaches Skyline Drive in 1.0 mile, at Mile 19.4 at the beginning of Keyser Run Fire Road; to the left, just down the road, the Pole Bridge Link Trail heads right to link with the Piney Branch Trail.) To complete this loop, go left on the fire road and stay straight past the Pole Bridge Link Trail. The road is blazed yellow for horse use.

As you descend the steep road, at 3.8 miles pass under a powerline and stay straight. On a more level area at 4.1 miles, watch for peculiarly twisted sassafras trees. At 4.3 miles pass the walled Bolen Cemetery on the left, where Dwyers, Tindalls, and Baileys are also buried, and reach a junction at 4.4 miles (to the right, the Hull School Trail leads south to the Piney Branch Trail, hike 14); stay left with the Keyser Run Fire Road.

The trail crisscrosses under the powerline a couple of times as it descends to the park boundary at 5.3 miles. Go around a chain blocking vehicle access, and continue down the road, which follows the park boundary on the left. You'll pass a private road up to the right and return to trailhead parking at 5.5 miles.

13   TUSCARORA/OVERALL RUN TRAIL

**Distance: 5.8 miles one-way; Overall Run Falls,
3.2 miles one-way**
Difficulty: Moderate
Elevation loss: 2,600 feet
Cautions: Rocky, steep descent
Connections: AT, Traces Nature Trail, Mathews Arm Trail,
Thompson Hollow Trail, Beecher-Overall Connecting Trail

Attractions: This hike down the western side of the Blue Ridge passes by the two falls of Overall Run, which bears the name of a family that owned the area for generations. The Tuscarora/Overall Run Trail was also called the "Big Blue Trail," but that name has recently been dropped. The Tuscarora Trail continues out of the park, west and north, for more than 200 miles to form a loop with the Appalachian Trail (AT), which it rejoins near Harrisburg, Pennsylvania. The name Tuscarora comes from an Indian tribe that lived in the area of Pennsylvania.

Trailhead: At Mile 21.1 on Skyline Drive, past the Hogback Overlook, turn into a paved parking area on the right, where you'll have access to the AT, which crosses the drive on the south end of the parking area.

Description: Take the AT to the right, headed south. You'll pass over one of the peaks of Hogback Mountain among witch hazel, small trees that bloom in fall with yellow flower clusters along the stems. At 0.4 mile, you reach a junction (the AT continues straight to cross Skyline Drive once again in another 0.6 mile); turn right on the Tuscarora/Overall Run Trail.

The trail winds down to a junction at 1.2 miles (to the left, a connector trail leads 0.1 mile to the Traces Nature Trail, hike 15, which circles the Mathews Arm Campground); turn right and stay on the Tuscarora/Overall Run Trail.

The trail ascends to then turn left, pass a large boulder, and wind down a steep, rocky slope. It bottoms out to cross a small stream in a wet area. The trail ascends again and reaches a junction at 2.7 miles (to the left, the Mathews Arm Trail, hike 16, is an old road that leads to the Mathews Arm Campground in 1.4 miles); stay to the right on the road. Here the two trails coincide for 0.1 mile; at 2.8 miles, where the Mathews Arm Trail goes straight, take the Tuscarora/Overall Run Trail off to the left.

You'll descend steeply to turn right along Overall Run. At 2.9 miles, a path to the left leads to a view of the 29-foot-high upper falls. Continue to descend on the steep, rocky path that winds down the mountain. At 3.2 miles the trail emerges onto rock outcrops that afford distant views of the 93-foot-high Overall Run Falls, sometimes called "Big Falls," the highest waterfall in the park. You'll also have a view down the valley of Overall Run.

The steep trail continues descending the ridge, crossing Overall Run and then crossing back, to a junction with the Thompson Hollow Trail at 5.2 miles. Here the Tuscarora and Overall Run Trails separate. (The Tuscarora turns right on the Thompson Hollow Trail, an old road. In 0.2 miles, the trail forks, with the Tuscarora Trail to the left and the Thompson Hollow Trail straight ahead, emerging from the park as VA 630. The Tuscarora continues west to cross a tributary of Overall Run, emerge from the park, and connect with US 340 at 2.8 miles.) Stay left on the Overall Run Trail.

Past the junction, the Overall Run Trail continues along the cascading Overall Run. At 5.8 miles it ends at a junction with the Beecher Ridge–Overall Run Connecting Trail. The Overall Run Trail ends at this junction because there is no longer access from outside the park.

(A loop can be hiked by turning left on the connecting trail, and then walking up the Beecher Ridge Trail to reconnect with the Mathews Arm Trail. Turning left there, you would close the loop at the junction with the Tuscarora/Overall Run Trail in 3.6 miles. There turn right to return to the AT and the parking area for a total of 12.1 miles.)

14 PINEY RIDGE, HULL SCHOOL, AND FORK MOUNTAIN TRAILS

Distance: 9.7-mile loop
Difficulty: Moderate
Elevation change: 1,500 feet
Cautions: Stream fords
Connections: AT, Piney Branch Trail

Attractions: This route follows old roads that descend along Piney River. In a meadow stands the Range View Cabin, built by the Potomac Appalachian Trail Club in the 1930s.

Trailhead: At Mile 22.1 on Skyline Drive, past the Rattlesnake Point Overlook, turn up a road on the left that leads to the Piney River Maintenance Area. Just before the maintenance area, stop at the parking area on the left. This was once the site of the Redbird Civilian Conservation Corps (CCC) Camp.

Description: From the parking area, walk up the road and turn left down a side road toward the Range View Cabin. At 0.1 mile, just before ranger housing, turn right off the paved road onto a gravel road to continue toward the cabin. At 0.2 mile, you reach a junction (the Appalachian Trail comes in from the left to join the road, and the Piney Branch Trail leads off to the left); continue straight down the road, with which the AT coincides. In a few paces the AT turns off left, but just continue straight down the road.

At 0.8 mile, the AT crosses the road; stay on the road. At 0.9 mile, the Piney Ridge Trail begins on the right (from here, the road curves left down to a meadow and the Range View Cabin); turn right onto the Piney Ridge Trail.

You'll pass through an old apple orchard and descend gently along the ridge. At 2.0 miles, in a gathering of white pine, old trees stand like ghosts in early morning fog. The trail descends an old roadway to a junction with the Fork Mountain Trail at 3.2 miles (this is the return route of the loop); turn left to continue on the Piney Ridge Trail.

The trail begins a steeper descent into the hollow of Piney River. It curves right in the descent through a more open area that was once a field or house site at 3.4 miles; piles of rock stand in the woods. Up from the clearing and down again, descend along an old roadway. A stream flows under rocks to make its way down to join Piney River below. At 4.2 miles, the Piney Ridge Trail ends at a junction with the Piney Branch Trail; turn right.

The trail descends along Piney River to a ford of the stream at 4.5 miles. The Hull School Trail comes in from the left to join the Piney Branch Trail at 4.6 miles (to the left, the Hull School Trail leads 0.7 mile to the Keyser Run Fire Road); stay to the right on the Piney Branch Trail/Hull School Trail.

You'll ford Piney River again at 4.8 miles. On the other side, the two trails split (the Piney Branch Trail leads left to continue down along Piney River, emerge from the park, and connect with VA 600 in another 1.9 miles); turn right on the Hull School Trail.

The trail ascends an old road, crosses a small stream, passes through an old rock wall and a pile of rocks from a cleared field, and ascends to a junction at 5.3 miles (the Hull School Trail continues straight down the old road to cross the Thornton River at the site of the old Hull School and emerge on Skyline Drive in another 2.9 miles); turn right off the Hull School Trail onto the Fork Mountain Trail.

Ascend through a hardwood forest in a steep ascent, eventually reaching the junction with the Piney Ridge Trail to close the loop at 6.5 miles. Stay straight for the 3.2 miles back to the Piney River Maintenance Area.

15 | TRACES NATURE TRAIL

Distance: 1.7-mile loop
Difficulty: Moderate
Elevation change: 200 feet
Cautions: Steep descent
Connections: Elkwallow Trail, Tuscarora/Overall Run Trail, Mathews Arm Trail

Attractions: This loop circles the Mathews Arm Campground while passing the traces of past human habitation. Numbered posts mark the sites of old roads, house sites, rock piles from cleared fields, rock fences, and forest plants. A metal box at the trailhead usually holds pamphlet guides to the numbered spots along the trail.

Trailhead: At Mile 22.2 on Skyline Drive, turn right into the Mathews

Arm Campground. The road descends steeply to the registration building in 0.7 mile. On the left side of the road, you'll see a post marking the beginning of the Elkwallow Trail (hike 18), which leads 2.0 miles to the Elkwallow Wayside. Turn right into a parking area for the amphitheater. At the far right end of the amphitheater parking, you'll find the trailhead for the Traces Nature Trail.

Description: Head into the woods. The trail ascends, frequently curving right and left, but mostly curving left as it circles the campground. At 0.5 mile, at post No. 9, a trail to the right leads 0.1 mile up to the Tuscarora/ Overall Run Trail; stay left on the Traces Nature Trail.

You'll descend steeply into a cove that was once a homesite with stone fences and a spring. At post No. 16, at 0.9 mile, you'll pass a fenced exclosure that keeps deer out so park staff can study the effects of browsing.

At 1.1 miles, the trail crosses a road that is the Mathews Arm Trail (to the left, it reaches the back end of the campground in 0.1 mile; to the right it is the route for hike 16); continue straight on the Traces Nature Trail.

You'll circle the large, rocky knoll at the back end of the campground, eventually passing under a powerline and emerging on the park road at 1.7 miles, behind the registration building and across from the amphitheater parking area.

16 | MATHEWS ARM TRAIL

Distance: 4.4 miles one-way
Difficulty: Moderate
Elevation loss: 1,300 feet
Cautions: Steep descent off ridge
Connections: Traces Nature Trail, Weddlewood Trail, Beecher Ridge Trail, Tuscarora/Overall Run Trail

Attractions: This old road serves to connect several trails behind the Mathews Arm Campground, giving access to the Weddlewood, Beecher Ridge, and Overall Run Trails, which can be combined for loop hikes out of the campground.

Trailhead: At Mile 22.2 on Skyline Drive, turn right into the Mathews Arm Campground. The road descends steeply to the registration building in 0.7 mile. Drive into the campground to the very back at a rocky knoll. The trail begins at the back of the campground; you'll see the gated old road to the right.

Description: The road circles left around the rocky knoll and descends to a junction with the Traces Nature Trail (hike 15) at 0.1 mile; continue straight up the old road as it runs along the ridge of Mathews Arm.

At 0.4 mile, you reach a junction (the Weddlewood Trail to the left connects with the Heiskell Hollow Trail, hike 17, which loops back to the campground in 2.5 miles); stay straight on the old road.

Continuing up the road, you reach a junction at 0.9 mile (the Beecher Ridge Trail to the left forms a 7.4-mile loop with the Heiskell Hollow Trail, and a 8.5-mile loop with the Overall Run Trail); stay straight.

The road swings to the right through the rocky streambed at the head of Overall Run and reaches a junction at 1.4 miles (the Tuscarora/Overall Run Trail, hike 13, comes in from the right); continue on the road, which bears left. At 1.5 miles the Tuscarora/Overall Run Trail turns off the road to the left; stay straight.

The Mathews Arm Trail continues out the ridge to eventually bear left in a steep descent, reaching the park boundary at 4.4 miles. (Access from there to VA 630 is difficult, so return the way you came.)

17 | MATHEWS ARM, WEDDLEWOOD, AND HEISKELL HOLLOW TRAILS

Distance: 2.9 miles one-way
Difficulty: Moderate
Elevation change: 600 feet
Cautions: None
Connections: Mathews Arm Trail, Knob Mountain Trail

Attractions: This pleasant walk offers connections for trails on the west end of Mathews Arm Campground and provides a short circuit route from the campground after you've set up camp for the night.

Trailhead: At Mile 22.2 on Skyline Drive, turn right into the Mathews Arm Campground. The road descends steeply to the registration building in 0.7 mile. Drive into the campground to the very back at a rocky knoll. The trail begins at the back of the campground; you'll see the gated old road to the right.

Description: Walk up the Mathews Arm Trail (hike 16) on the road, which circles left around the rocky knoll and descends to a junction with the Traces Nature Trail (hike 15) at 0.1 mile; continue straight up the old road as it runs along the ridge of Mathews Arm.

At 0.4 mile you reach the junction with the Weddlewood Trail to the left (the old road goes straight, hike 16); turn left onto the Weddlewood Trail.

The trail descends following an old roadbed. The road swings left and descends more steeply, eventually reaching a junction with the Heiskell Hollow Trail at 1.7 miles. (To the right, the Heiskell Hollow Trail descends to the west, following the East Fork, to emerge from the park on VA 697 in 3.2 miles, but access there is difficult and not recommended; you can make a 7.4-mile loop by turning right down the Heiskell Hollow Trail for 1.8 miles and then turning right on the Beecher Ridge Trail to return to the Mathews Arm Trail for the walk back to the campground.) Continue straight on the road, which is now the Heiskell Hollow Trail leading toward the campground.

Ascend the rocky roadbed to reach a junction at 2.5 miles with a gravel road (to the right it leads to the wastewater treatment plant; this is also the Knob Mountain Trail, which in several yards turns off this road to head south along Knob Mountain and connect with the Jeremys Run Trail in 7.1 miles, hike 18); turn left on the gravel road.

At 2.9 miles you'll emerge on a paved road that leads straight into the campground.

18 | JEREMYS RUN, KNOB MOUNTAIN, AND ELKWALLOW TRAILS

Distance: 5.2-mile loop
Difficulty: Moderate
Elevation change: 700 feet
Cautions: Creek ford, steep ascent
Connections: AT, Heiskell Hollow Trail

Attractions: This circuit hike introduces several backcountry trails and provides access to Jeremys Run, one of the prettiest streams in the park, before ascending to the top of Knob Mountain.

Trailhead: On Skyline Drive, after passing the Elkwallow Wayside, turn into the Elkwallow Picnic Area at Mile 24.1 on the right; the road is one-way. At the back end of the picnic area lies the trailhead for Jeremys Run and the AT.

Description: From the picnic area, head straight into the woods on the Jeremys Run Trail. In 200 feet you'll connect with the Appalachian Trail (AT) (your return route will be along the AT from the right); turn left as the AT and Jeremys Run Trail coincide.

At 0.2 mile, a spring lies on the left. Descending, you reach a junction at 0.3 mile (the AT turns left, heading south toward Thornton Gap); stay straight on Jeremys Run Trail.

The trail curves right in a descent and at 0.5 mile curves left to cross a shallow stream. The stream flows below on your right. At 0.7 mile the trail joins an old roadbed, where you bear to the left on the roadway. Continuing to descend, you'll see the convergence of two streams below that form Jeremys Run. At 0.8 mile, descend to a junction with the Knob Mountain Cutoff Trail on the right. (Jeremys Run Trail continues straight on the old roadway down the gorge of Jeremys Run, crossing the stream many times in the descent, eventually emerging from the park in 5.4 miles and soon after connecting with VA 611. Toward the end, Jeremys Run Trail connects with the Neighbor Mountain Trail to form a 13.9-mile loop hike with the AT; just after, Jeremys Run Trail connects with the lower end of the Knob Mountain Trail to form an 11.4-mile loop to the west.) Turn right on the Knob Mountain Cutoff Trail.

The trail swings right and drops to a ford of Jeremys Run. It then begins a steep ascent of Knob Mountain with switchbacks. Near the top, pass through a gap in a long rock fence that once enclosed a field or marked a boundary. The trail then curves to the right to a junction at 1.3 miles at the crest of the ridge where the Knob Mountain Trail follows an old roadway (to the left in 2.2 miles stands one of the summits of the mountain); turn right toward the Mathews Arm Campground.

The old roadway ascends as it winds its way up the ridge, eventually curving right to swing around the taller summit of Knob Mountain. At 2.8 miles, emerge on a road that leads down from the Mathews Arm Campground (to the left it leads to a water treatment plant); turn to the right up the road. Soon after, the Heiskell Hollow Trail (hike 17) joins the road from the left; stay straight on the road.

At 3.2 miles, you'll connect with a turnaround and parking area for access from the campground to the Knob Mountain Trail. Walk up the road into the campground to turn right on the entrance road past the registration building. Then watch for the Elkwallow Trail on the right at 3.4 miles; take this trail.

The Elkwallow Trail first follows an old roadway up from the paved road, but in a few paces turns off the roadway on a path to the right. The trail winds down to skirt a small stream, which runs out of the campground, and then follows the stream down in a steep descent to a boardwalk crossing of the upper reaches of Jeremys Run at 3.7 miles. Up from the creek crossing, the trail merges with an old roadway and parallels Skyline Drive, which is out of sight, to a junction with the AT at 4.7 miles. (To the left the AT crosses Skyline Drive to head north; straight ahead, you can reach the Elkwallow Wayside in another 0.1 mile.) To complete this loop hike, turn right on the AT.

The trail descends and then climbs to intersect with the Jeremys Run Trail and close the loop at 5.2 miles. Turn left to get back to parking at the Elkwallow Picnic Area.

19 | THORNTON RIVER TRAIL

Distance: 4.9 miles one-way; Thornton River, 1.5 miles one-way
Difficulty: Moderate
Elevation loss: 1,200 feet
Cautions: Stream fords
Connections: AT, Hull School Trail

Attractions: The trail descends along the North Fork of the Thornton River, offering a pleasant stroll through an area once frequented by mountaineers. The numerous rock piles you see in the woods remain from the clearing of fields for growing crops. Thornton Hollow is wide and covered with thick grass dotted with pink, white, and yellow flowers along a small stream that is a tributary of the Thornton River. The trail could become overgrown in late summer.

Trailhead: Turn into the trailhead parking area on the east side of Skyline Drive at Mile 25.4. Just to the south of this parking area, the Thornton River Trail heads west up the slope to connect with the Appalachian Trail (AT) in 0.3 mile. For this hike, take the Thornton River Trail east down the ridge following an old road that begins at the left side of the parking area.

Description: Descend along the dirt road, which passes below the parking area and curves left to descend into Thornton Hollow. At 0.1 mile rockhop a small stream. At 0.5 mile the road curves left and passes a spring on the left at 0.6 mile. Watch for a pile of rocks to the left at 0.8 mile that's the first sign of former human habitation in the hollow.

Cross a small stream from a spring at 1.0 mile, and then at 1.1 miles pass an old rusted car abandoned on the left. Soon after, watch for the trail to turn left. At 1.3 miles you'll cross another small stream from a spring to the left.

To the right at 1.4 miles, the small tributary you have been following joins the North Fork of the Thornton River. At 1.5 miles, you'll pass through rock walls and turn down to the right to ford the Thornton River, not very wide even though it's called a "river" at this point.

The trail continues to follow the river, fording the stream three times before reaching a junction with the Hull School Trail at 3.1 miles. (Hull School once stood near this intersection; to the left, the Hull School Trail ascends to a junction with the Fork Mountain Trail in 0.7 mile; to the right, the Hull School Trail ascends 2.2 miles to Skyline Drive at Mile 28.2.) The Thornton River Trail continues straight through the junction to emerge from the park at 4.9 miles along an old road that becomes VA 612; parking is very limited there.

20 | BYRDS NEST NO. 4 LOOP

Distance: 2.5 miles
Difficulty: Moderate
Elevation change: 300 feet
Cautions: Steep ascent
Connections: Neighbor Mountain Trail, Hull School Trail, AT

Attractions: This short loop starts at Beahms Gap, named for a family that entered the region around 1750, and takes you by Byrds Nest No. 4 day-use shelter. There are four such shelters in the park; the money for their construction was donated by Harry F. Byrd Sr., who was Virginia's governor during the formation of the park and led the effort to raise funds for the purchase of the land; he was later U.S. Senator from Virginia. Byrds Nest No. 4 was built in 1965.

Trailhead: Start at Beahms Gap at Mile 28.5, where you'll find parking on the right side of Skyline Drive.

Description: On the north end of the parking area, take the trail leading into the woods, which descends to the Appalachian Trail (AT) at 0.1 mile; turn right on the AT.

At 0.2 mile, the trail crosses an old roadway marked by rows of rocks on your left. Just beyond, there's a spring off to your left. Beyond that is a junction (the AT goes left, your return route); stay straight on a connector trail.

Ascend to connect with the service road up to Byrds Nest No. 4 at 0.4 mile (to the right on the service road, you can descend 0.1 mile to emerge on Skyline Drive across from the access to the Hull School Trail); turn left on the service road, which is also the Neighbor Mountain Trail.

Make a steep ascent to enter a clearing at 0.8 mile, where you'll find Byrds Nest No. 4 day-use shelter. The Neighbor Mountain Trail passes beside the shelter on the right to ascend over the ridge and begin a descent of the mountain on the other side. At 1.3 miles you reach a junction (a side trail to the right leads 0.3 mile to reach Skyline Drive and trail access parking at Mile 26.8); stay straight on the Neighbor Mountain Trail.

At 1.4 miles, you reach an intersection with the AT. (To the right, the AT descends steeply to pass the parking area on Skyline Drive at Mile 26.8, where a short trail connects the AT with the parking area at the same point at which the Neighbor Mountain Trail connector reaches the parking area; the Neighbor Mountain Trail continues straight to run out along the ridge of Neighbor Mountain, topping the summit, and then bearing north to descend off the mountain to a junction with the Jeremys Run Trail in 4.6 miles—the Neighbor Mountain and Jeremys Run Trails and the AT can be combined for a 13.9-mile loop hike.) Turn left to follow the AT to the southeast to complete this short loop hike.

The AT passes over a knoll and begins a descent off the ridge of Neighbor

Byrds Nest No. 4 (Photo by John Amberson, courtesy of Shenandoah National Park)

Mountain. Descend into a saddle between Neighbor Mountain and Byrds Nest Summit, and then bear to the right around the summit while descending through numerous large rock outcrops. At 2.3 miles, close the loop at the junction with the connector trail to the left that leads to the Neighbor Mountain Trail, where it coincides with the Byrds Nest No. 4 service road; turn right on the AT to return to Beahms Gap at 2.5 miles.

(You can continue on the AT around the parking area at Beahms Gap to emerge on Skyline Drive just to the south of the parking area, which will add another 0.1 mile to your walk.)

21 | PASS MOUNTAIN

Distance: 1.0 mile one-way
Difficulty: Moderate
Elevation gain: 550 feet
Cautions: Steady ascent
Connections: Rocky Branch Trail, AT

Attractions: This hike ascends to the summit of Pass Mountain among rock outcrops and a grand view to the west of Neighbor and Knob Mountains.

Trailhead: Begin at the Beahms Gap parking area on the right at Mile 28.5.

Description: Just to the south of the gap parking area, pick up the Appalachian Trail (AT) where it crosses Skyline Drive. On the east side of the drive, follow the AT as it continues south.

At 0.1 mile, the AT crosses the Rocky Branch Trail. (To the left, this trail travels 0.4 mile to emerge at the parking for the Hull School Trail on Skyline Drive at Mile 28.2; to the right, the Rocky Branch Trail continues south to cross Skyline Drive and reach the park boundary in 2.8 miles on VA 666.) Continue straight on the AT through the intersection with the Rocky Branch Trail.

Soon the trail curves right and begins an ascent of Pass Mountain. As the trail winds its way up the mountain, it doglegs to the right at 0.6 mile and then again at 0.7 mile. The trail is then somewhat level. As you begin ascending again, the AT makes another dogleg to the right, closer to the edge of the mountain.

Just as you top a shoulder of the mountain, the trail passes through rocks at 0.9 mile. There's some view through the trees, but stay on the trail to the far end of the outcrop, where a path leads to the right to a view on the west of Kemp Hollow, with Neighbor Mountain to the right and Knob Mountain beyond. Across this second shoulder, the AT then switchbacks up through rocks to the summit of Pass Mountain at 1.0 mile.

(The AT swings left across the summit, and then begins a descent of the other side of Pass Mountain. If you choose to continue on, at 1.8 miles you reach the Pass Mountain Trail, which descends east past the Pass Mountain Hut and emerges in 3 miles on US 211 east of Thornton Gap; there is some parking across the highway. The AT continues past the Pass Mountain Trail to descend into Thornton Gap at 3.1 miles.)

CENTRAL DISTRICT

Marys Rock

The Central District includes the park area from Thornton Gap to Swift Run Gap. This is the most popular of the three districts because it contains the park's two lodges—Skyland Lodge, originally George Pollock's resort which helped inspire the creation of Shenandoah National Park, and Big Meadows Lodge, located at the scenic Big Meadows, an open area on the crest of the mountains frequented by wildlife. The Central District also includes the Big Meadows and Lewis Mountain Campgrounds and the Big Meadows Wayside, in addition to the Byrd Visitor Center and four picnic areas (Pinnacles, Big Meadows, Lewis Mountain, and South River). The peaks of the Central District include The Pinnacle, Stony Man and Hawksbill Mountains, Old Rag, and Hazeltop and Bearfence Mountains. The Central District is described in six sections: Thornton Gap to Skyland, the Skyland area, Skyland to Big Meadows, the Big Meadows area, Big Meadows to Lewis Mountain, and Lewis Mountain to Swift Run Gap.

THORNTON GAP TO SKYLAND

The Central District begins at Thornton Gap, which can be reached from the west on US 211, from New Market, which is on I-81, and Luray. From the east, US 211 heads into the park from Sperryville and "Little" Washington. At the park entrance stands the Thornton Gap Entrance Station. Coming from the North District, Skyline Drive dips through Thornton Gap and continues south into the Central District; Marys Rock stands at the top of the gap on the south side.

To reach the trailheads farther south that are only accessible from outside the park on the east (see hikes 34, 35, and 44 in the Skyland to Big Meadows section), you need to exit Skyline Drive at Mile 31.5 here in Thornton Gap. Descend east on US 211. Turn south on US 522 in Sperryville, then south again on VA 231, to reach trailhead parking on Berry Hollow Fire Road and Weakley Hollow Fire Road.

At the time the park was established, there was a Panorama Hotel and Restaurant in Thornton Gap. The name "Panorama" apparently dates from a house of Andrew Russell Barbee, who operated the road through the gap as a toll road. Now there's the Panorama Restaurant and Giftshop, built in the 1960s and operated by the concessionaire. At times, park information and backcountry camping permits are available at the small building to the front, which is only intermittently staffed.

This northernmost portion of the Central District includes Stony Man Mountain. Looking south from the Stony Man Mountain Overlook, you can see the profile of Stony Man; the rock bluff on the mountain forms his brow, an outcrop serves as his nose, the trees down the slope form his flowing beard. When you hike to the summit of Stony Man Mountain, you'll be standing on a rock ledge at the top of his forehead. In addition to Stony Man, hikes in this northern portion of the Central District lead to Marys Rock, White Rocks, The Pinnacle, Corbin Cabin, and Millers Head.

Skyline Drive: South from US 211 at Thornton Gap, Skyline Drive at Mile 32.2 passes through 600-foot Marys Rock Tunnel. From the Tunnel Parking Overlook at Mile 32.4 on the left, Thornton River Hollow is below, with Oventop Mountain to the left and Skinner Ridge to the right. Out through the hollow lies Sperryville, near where Thornton Mill once stood.

At the Buck Hollow Overlook on the left at Mile 32.9, Skinner Ridge lies below, with Buck Hollow to the right and Buck Ridge farther to the right; you can just see Hazel Mountain over Buck Ridge. At the Hazel Mountain

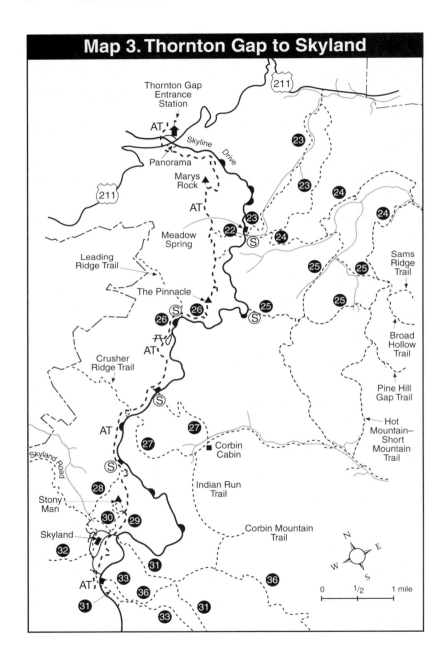

Map 3. Thornton Gap to Skyland

Thornton Gap
Entrance
Station

AT

Skyline

Drive

211

Panorama

Marys
Rock

AT

23

23

24

24

23

22

24

S

Meadow
Spring

Leading
Ridge Trail

The Pinnacle

25

25

Sams
Ridge
Trail

25

25

26

26

25

S

S

Broad
Hollow
Trail

AT

Crusher
Ridge Trail

Pine Hill
Gap Trail

AT

S

Hot
Mountain–
Short
Mountain
Trail

AT

27

27

Corbin
Cabin

S

Indian Run
Trail

28

Stony
Man

Skyland Road

30

29

Corbin Mountain
Trail

Skyland

32

31

36

AT

33

36

36

N

31

36

E

W

31

33

31

S

0   1/2   1 mile

Overlook at Mile 33.0, you can climb up granodiorite boulders for a view across Buck Hollow to Buck Ridge, with Hazel Mountain on the other side. Meadow Spring parking area is at Mile 33.5, where you can access the Meadow Spring Trail (hike 22) to Marys Rock, the Buck Hollow Trail (hike 23) for a loop with the Buck Ridge Trail, and the Hazel Mountain Trail (hike 24) for access to White Rocks.

Continuing south from Meadow Spring parking, the service road for Byrds Nest No. 3 shelter is on the right at Mile 33.9. Then the Pinnacles Overlook on the left at Mile 35.1 offers a view of Hannah Run Valley below, framed by Catlett Mountain to the left and Pinnacle Ridge to the right, with Old Rag Mountain in the background. Here you can access the Hannah Run Trail (hike 25).

From the Pinnacles Overlook south on Skyline Drive, the pinxter-flower is especially plentiful; the pink blossoms of this azalea decorate the edge of the forest along the drive in late May. The Jewell Hollow Overlook lies on the right side of Skyline Drive at Mile 36.4, where you can pick up the Appalachian Trail (AT) for a hike to The Pinnacle (hike 26).

At Mile 36.7, the Pinnacles Picnic Area lies on the right. The AT skirts the back end of the picnic area; 100 yards south on the AT, you can walk to a viewpoint that was becoming overgrown the last time I was there, but it may be cleared by now.

A parking area on the right side of Skyline Drive at Mile 37.9 provides access to Corbin Cabin (hike 27).

At Mile 38.4, the Nicholson Hollow Trail emerges on Skyline Drive from the left and then, just beyond, reenters the woods on the other side.

Skyline Drive then reaches the Stony Man Mountain Overlook at Mile 38.6 with the profile of Stony Man to the south. Straight out from this overlook, you can see the town of Luray and, beyond, New Market Gap in Massanutten Mountain. North from the overlook stands The Pinnacle. A short trail at the southern end of the parking area leads past rest rooms to connect with the AT.

A parking area on the right at Mile 39.1 provides additional access to the Appalachian Trail, from which you can access the Passamaquoddy Trail (hike 28). From the Hemlock Springs Overlook on the left at Mile 39.7, you'll have a view north into Nicholson Hollow, with The Pinnacle to the left and Hazel and Catlett Mountains to the right. Hemlock Springs lies below the overlook, out of sight.

The view from the Thorofare Mountain Overlook at Mile 40.5 is probably the most photographed scene in the park. A tall dead tree out from the overlook frames Old Rag Mountain in the distance, the exposed granite at the mountain peak making it look ragged. Thorofare Mountain lies straight out from the overlook.

At Mile 41.7, a road to the right is the north entrance to Skyland.

22 | MARYS ROCK VIA MEADOW SPRING TRAIL AND AT

Distance: 1.4 miles one-way
Difficulty: Moderate
Elevation gain: 600 feet
Cautions: Steep ascent, drop-offs
Connections: AT

Attractions: Marys Rock on the Appalachian Trail (AT), just north of the Meadow Spring Trail, provides a panoramic view of Thornton Gap. Marys Rock was named for either the daughter of Frances Thornton, for whom the gap is named, or the wife of William Randolph Barbee, son of Andrew Barbee, who managed the toll road through Thornton Gap; William took over the toll road from his father and was later a famous sculptor, as was his son, Herbert. Just south of the Meadow Spring Trail is Byrds Nest No. 3 shelter, built in 1963 with funds provided by Senator Harry F. Byrd Sr. In spring watch for blooming laurel and azalea and stands of cinnamon fern along this trail.

Trailhead: Continue south on Skyline Drive past Panorama, and turn into the Meadow Spring parking area on the left at Mile 33.5.

(You can also reach Marys Rock along the AT from the Panorama complex in Thornton Gap; at the end of the upper parking lot, you'll find a short connector trail to the AT, which you can then take south for a steep ascent of the mountain, reaching Marys Rock in 1.7 miles.)

Description: From the parking area, walk north up Skyline Drive 100 yards and cross to the beginning of the Meadow Spring Trail, marked by a post on the west side of the road. You'll pass a stream on the right descending from Meadow Spring.

The trail leads into the woods in a steep ascent. At 0.4 mile, pass the foundation and chimney for a backcountry cabin that burned in the 1940s. At 0.7 mile, the Meadow Spring Trail ascends to a junction with the Appalachian Trail (to the left, the AT passes Byrds Nest No. 3 shelter in 0.6 mile and reaches Skyland in 7.1 miles); turn right to get to Marys Rock.

There's a view from rocks to the left at 1.1 miles. Continuing north, the AT curves around a rock monolith at 1.3 miles and reaches a junction soon after (the AT turns right); turn left here onto a side path leading to Marys Rock. Ascend to Marys Rock at 1.4 miles. Standing on the bare rock of the summit, old rock of Pedlar granodiorite, you have an expansive view of Thornton Gap 1,200 feet below.

(From Marys Rock you can return the way you came to the Meadow Spring parking area, or if you have a vehicle to pick you up at Thornton

Chimney of a backcountry cabin that burned in the 1940s

Gap, you can descend on the AT to Panorama. In making the descent, you'll drop below rock outcrops at 2.1 miles, walk some sections of trail shored up with stone cribbing, and make several switchbacks to reach a junction at 3.1 miles; the AT heads straight through Thornton Gap to continue north, but take the trail to the right, which leads 30 yards out to the upper parking lot at the Panorama Restaurant.)

23

BUCK HOLLOW AND BUCK RIDGE TRAILS

Distance: 5.6-mile loop
Difficulty: Moderate; strenuous ascent
Elevation change: 1,750 feet
Cautions: Steep descent and ascent, stream fords
Connections: Meadow Spring Trail, Hazel Mountain Trail

Attractions: This loop hike descends along a pretty stream with boulders and cascades, and then ascends along a ridge with views of Thornton Gap. Watch for early spring wildflowers, sprinklings of blue hepatica, in the wet stream areas. The dry ridgeline has a pine, laurel, and oak forest.

Trailhead: Begin at the Meadow Spring parking area on the left at Mile 33.5 on Skyline Drive; you can access the Meadow Spring Trail (hike 22) on the other side of the road.

Description: At the right end of the parking area, where the Hazel Mountain Trail (hike 24) heads straight down an old road, the Buck Hollow Trail turns off left to pass behind the parking area. The trail soon swings right and heads straight out, descending gently. At 0.1 mile the trail skirts the stream that flows down from Meadow Spring on your right.

The trail descends more steeply at 0.3 mile as the stream drops more rapidly down Buck Hollow. At 0.7 mile the trail turns right, where you'll need to rockhop the now-tumbling stream. As the trail continues downstream on your left, it passes several cascades; watch for a multistep drop in the streambed at 1.0 mile.

The trail stays up for a time and then at 1.1 miles curves right to begin the descent again. The trail becomes steep and rocky as it winds down into the hollow.

Back along the creek, watch for a natural water slide in the streambed at 1.7 miles. At 1.8 miles, the trail swings right to cross a side stream and immediately turns left to ford the main stream; do not go straight on an old roadbed.

As you continue to descend along the stream, now on your right, the trail crosses wet-weather streams and springs. At 2.5 miles, bear left across a shallow side stream, which may be dry in summer, to continue down a rocky section of trail. Swing right and ford the main creek, which has grown larger, at 2.7 miles.

At 2.8 miles is a junction with the Buck Ridge Trail on the right. (The Buck Hollow Trail continues along the creek to ford it again and then ford the Thornton River, emerging on US 211; there's a pulloff and room to park a few cars on this east side of the Blue Ridge down from Thornton Gap.) To complete this loop hike, take the sharp right onto the Buck Ridge Trail.

Cross a side stream and walk up a rocky and usually dry streambed, and then bear left out of the streambed to begin a steep ascent of Buck Ridge at 2.9 miles. The trail soon bears right and keeps climbing in a long, tough ascent that's about as steep as it gets without having to use your hands to pull yourself up. At 3.0 miles, you reach the ridgeline and continue in a more gentle ascent, with some steep sections.

At 3.9 miles, the trail swings to the north side of the ridge, where you'll step down a rock outcrop that's a perfect resting place offering a view through the trees of Thornton Gap; Skinner Ridge lies to the left and Pass Mountain stands across the gap, with Oventop Mountain to the right. As you continue around the bluff, you'll be looking at Marys Rock over Skinner Ridge. The trail soon swings left back to the ridgeline and continues the ascent.

Top a shoulder of the ridge at 4.1 miles and continue along the ridgeline, with Skinner Ridge to the right and Hazel Mountain to the left. At 4.5 miles, the trail makes a winding ascent of a rocky slope. Soon, a side path leads to a limited view east. At 4.6 miles, the trail curves across bare rock through an open area that offers winter views through leafless trees.

Later, skirting to the left of the ridgeline, there's a junction at 5.1 miles with an old road that's the Hazel Mountain Trail (hike 24); turn right. You'll return to the Meadow Spring parking area to close the loop at 5.6 miles.

24 | HAZEL MOUNTAIN, WHITE ROCKS, AND HAZEL RIVER TRAILS

Distance: 8.4-mile loop; Hazel River Falls, 2.5 miles one-way; White Rocks, 3.0 miles one-way
Difficulty: Moderate
Elevation change: 1,400 feet
Cautions: Steep descent to waterfall, stream crossings
Connections: Buck Hollow Trail, Buck Ridge Trail, Catlett Spur Trail

Attractions: Once on the White Rocks Trail, you'll have access to a picturesque waterfall and the White Rocks, exposed Old Rag granite. The return portion reaches the Hazel River before ascending Hazel Mountain.

Trailhead: The Hazel Mountain Trail begins at the Meadow Spring parking area on the left at Mile 33.5 on Skyline Drive.

Description: Just to the right of the parking area, the Hazel Mountain Trail follows an old road (the Buck Hollow Trail turns off to the left to pass below the parking area and head north); stay straight on the old road past a chain gate. The water from Meadow Spring runs under the trail in a culvert.

Descending along the road, you'll reach a junction at 0.5 mile (the Buck Ridge Trail, hike 23, is to the left); bear to the right.

As you continue to descend, the footing becomes rocky on the old roadway. At 0.7 mile the road curves left and, at 1.1 miles, curves back right. At 1.4 miles, you'll see a stream off to the right, a tributary of the Hazel River. At 1.5 miles, rockhop a side stream of this tributary and pass a hemlock woods along the creek. You reach a junction at 1.6 miles with the White Rocks Trail to the left (the Hazel Mountain Trail, the return route for this loop hike, continues straight); turn left onto the White Rocks Trail.

Ascend another old roadway that is the Old Hazel Road, crossing a small stream and reaching a dry ridge of oak and laurel. The trail gradually bears right and begins a descent along the ridgeline. Across the valley of the Hazel River, you'll see Hazel Mountain off to the right. At 2.4 miles, there's a path to the right that hikers have made looking for the waterfall, but this is not the trail to the falls. Continue descending on the old roadway. At 2.5 miles you'll reach a more worn path to the right that gives access to the waterfall; when I was last there, a tree snag with a trail blaze stood at the junction.

Although the walk to this junction has been easy, the path down to the waterfall is difficult. You need to be agile to make the steep descent to the Hazel River and then to make your way upstream to the 8-foot falls, which is worth the 0.2-mile scramble. At the falls, an overhang to the right shelters a crevice opening a few feet into the rock.

Back on the main trail, continue down the old road. You'll pass exposed boulders and dip through a saddle to then make an ascent of the first of three knolls along the ridge. At 2.8 miles, top the first knoll and then descend the other side. Hazel Mountain stands mightily to the right, and you'll hear the Hazel River below. Through another saddle and up the second knoll, watch for large patches of trailing arbutus. You'll have nice views left across the valley to Buck Ridge.

The trail skirts to the left of the peak of the second knoll, which is topped by the White Rocks. You'll only catch a glimpse of the rocks from the trail. But keep going, and on the other side of the knoll at 3.0 miles, just before the trail begins the descent into the next saddle, a path to the right takes you up into the giant exposed boulders.

The White Rocks Trail continues down and then over a third knoll before turning right to descend off the ridge. The trail then fords the Hazel River and crosses a tributary to connect with the Hazel River Trail at 3.9 miles (to the left, the Hazel River Trail exits the park in 1.2 miles to connect with VA 600); turn right up the Hazel River Trail.

Reconnect with the Hazel Mountain Trail at 5.5 miles (to the left, the Hazel Mountain Trail gives access to several backcountry trails and ends at a junction with the Pine Hill Gap Trail in another 2.9 miles); turn right.

Ford Runyon Run, pass the Catlett Spur Trail to the left, and cross the Hazel River on a bridge to close the loop at the beginning of the White Rocks Trail at 6.8 miles; stay straight. It's then another 1.6 miles back to Meadow Spring parking, at 8.4 miles.

25 | HANNAH RUN AND CATLETT MOUNTAIN TRAILS

Distance: 6.4-mile loop
Difficulty: Moderate
Elevation change: 1,100 feet
Cautions: Stream crossings
Connections: Hazel Mountain Trail, Hazel River Trail, Sams Ridge Trail/Broad Hollow Trail

Attractions: This loop hike introduces you to a section of the Shenandoah wilderness, passing along Runyon Run, a tributary of the Hazel River, and ascending Catlett Mountain.

Trailhead: Turn in at the Pinnacles Overlook on the left at Mile 35.1. Look to the far left of the parking area for a trailhead post and a gap in the rock wall. You'll descend stone steps there and bear left to begin the Hannah Run Trail.

Description: Descending a few yards, the trail switchbacks to the right through some rocks, but soon turns left. Hiking the trail in the fall, you'll find bright leaves littering the ground like the remains of a parade that has passed through.

The trail winds down the ridge, dips through a couple of coves, and then heads out onto a ridge. Descend from the ridge and switchback left to a junction at 1.2 miles (here the Hannah Run Trail continues to the right to connect with the Nicholson Hollow Trail in another 2.5 miles); for this loop hike, turn left onto the Catlett Mountain Trail.

At 1.3 miles, there's a second junction (the Catlett Mountain Trail continues straight, which will be your return route); to walk this loop clockwise, turn left here on the Catlett Spur Trail. This trail follows an old roadway, on and off. At 1.9 miles, a hemlock grove stands on the left.

At 2.0 miles at Runyon Run, a tributary of the Hazel River, turn right downstream. The trail crosses a small tributary where the stream joins the creek. Then rockhop Runyon Run at 2.1 miles and turn downstream. The trail crosses another small tributary and passes through a wet area where a spring emerges on the left. Watch for rows and piles of rocks along a section of old roadway, evidence of past settlement. Descend to a junction beside Runyon Run at 2.4 miles (the Hazel Mountain Trail straight ahead ascends back to Skyline Drive, passing the White Rocks Trail, hike 24); turn right on the Hazel Mountain Trail.

Ford Runyon Run and head up an old road along a tributary. You'll ascend steeply to reach a junction at 3.4 miles (the Hazel River Trail to the left descends along the Hazel River, passing the other end of the White Rocks Trail, to emerge from the park on a road and connect with VA 600 in 2.8 miles); stay straight on the Hazel Mountain Trail.

The trail reaches a junction at 3.5 miles. (The Sams Ridge Trail/Broad Hollow Trail is to the left; these two trails separate in another 0.2 mile, and each descends the ridge.) Continue straight up the old roadway.

Descend to a junction with the Catlett Mountain Trail at 4.0 miles (the Hazel Mountain Trail continues straight, to end at junctions with the Hot Mountain–Short Mountain and the Pine Hill Gap Trails); turn right on the Catlett Mountain Trail.

The trail descends through pine and hemlock. At 4.1 miles, a wagon wheel rim lay on the ground between two stream crossings when I last hiked through here. The trail ascends from these streams. At 4.2 miles, notice rock piles to the left that mark the site of a house or field. The trail then bears right to wind uphill.

After crossing this spur ridge of Catlett Mountain, the trail descends, skirts left around a sinkhole, and closes the loop at the junction with the Catlett Spur Trail on the right at 5.1 miles; stay straight.

At 5.2 miles reach the Hannah Run Trail (straight ahead it connects with the Nicholson Hollow Trail in 2.5 miles); turn right to return to Skyline Drive at the Pinnacles Overlook at 6.4 miles.

26 | THE PINNACLE VIA THE AT

Distance: 1.2 miles one-way
Difficulty: Moderate
Elevation gain: 350 feet
Cautions: Rocky in places
Connections: AT, Leading Ridge Trail

Attractions: A short hike on the Appalachian Trail (AT) takes you over The Pinnacle, the fifth-highest peak in the park at 3,720 feet, for a view to the northwest of Marys Rock and Jewell Hollow. At the summit, boulders stand on end, contributing to the name "Pinnacle."

Trailhead: Pull into the Jewell Hollow Overlook on the right at Mile 36.4, and park at the back of the second parking area. The view is of Tutweiler Hollow straight out from the overlook, bounded by Leading Ridge on the right. The valley beyond Leading Ridge is Jewell Hollow.

Description: At the back of the parking area, you'll find a 50-foot path that connects with the Appalachian Trail (the Pinnacles Picnic Area is 0.3 mile to the left along the AT); turn right to hike to The Pinnacle.

The AT descends right and left down to a broad shelf that it traverses below the overlook parking area. At 0.2 mile you'll pass a side path to the right that offers a second way for you to access the AT from the overlook, this one from the first parking area.

The trail then passes through an open area with a view down Tutweiler Hollow. Back into the woods, begin an ascent of Leading Ridge. At 0.3 mile, you reach an intersection with the Leading Ridge Trail. (To the right, the trail emerges on Skyline Drive in 0.1 mile at Mile 36.2—there's no parking; to the left, the trail leads out Leading Ridge to dead-end at the park boundary in 1.2 miles.) Continue straight ahead on the AT.

From Leading Ridge, continue ascending, passing through a laurel thicket. At 0.7 mile, ascend among huge granodiorite boulders of the Pedlar Formation. A pile of boulders on the left at 0.8 mile has one about 15 feet high standing on end. You'll soon pass over a shoulder of the ridge and continue along the ridgeline. At 1.0 mile the trail passes over the first summit of The Pinnacle. The trail descends a little, where you'll pass more boulders standing on end. You then ascend over the northern summit of The Pinnacle.

The AT begins a descent from The Pinnacle with switchbacks right and left. At 1.2 miles, after the AT turns right again, watch for a path on the left that leads out to a point surrounded in trees. You can climb on rocks for a view north to Marys Rock and to the northwest down Jewell Hollow with Neighbor Mountain in the distance. (From here, the AT continues to descend, passing Byrds Nest No. 3 shelter in another 0.8 mile and a junction with the Meadow Spring Trail, hike 22, in 0.6 mile beyond the shelter.)

27 | CORBIN CABIN, NICHOLSON HOLLOW, AND AT

Distance: 4.2-mile loop
Difficulty: Moderate
Elevation change: 1,050 feet
Cautions: Steep descent and ascent, rocky
Connections: AT, Indian Run Trail, Crusher Ridge Trail

Attractions: This short loop takes you by the historic Corbin Cabin and provides access to the backcountry; the forest has mountain laurel, pinxterflower, and patches of pink lady's slipper; in spring the path is pretty in pink. Several families in Nicholson Hollow once formed "Free State Hollow," where they were free to govern their own lives, since the law feared to enter. Aaron Nicholson, the patriarch of the community, was by most accounts a formidable person with his white beard and piercing blue eyes.

Corbin Cabin, built by George Corbin in 1909, is one of the last remaining examples of the mountaineer cabins. The original intent of the National Park Service was to preserve several historic structures after the park was established; an early report identified more than forty structures that represented the agricultural, mining, and lumbering practices of the early century. But at the time, resources were limited. The young men of the Civilian Conservation Corps camps were busy developing new visitor facilities. Then World War II intervened. The buildings were left, virtually abandoned, while resources went elsewhere. By the late 1940s, the only structure originally identified that could be salvaged was the Corbin Cabin. The Potomac Appalachian Trail Club took up the task and restored the structure in the 1950s. The PATC maintains the cabin today; it may be rented for overnight stays.

Trailhead: Pull into the parking area on the right side of Skyline Drive at Mile 37.9.

Description: At the south end of the parking area, a path leads a short distance to the AT; this is your return route. To start the hike, walk across Skyline Drive and pick up the Corbin Cabin Cutoff Trail.

The trail descends through the woods, making a steep descent, curving left at 0.6 mile, and turning down to the right along a small stream at 0.7 mile. Watch for a large oak tree on the left at 0.8 mile.

At 1.0 mile, a rock pile from a cleared field stands on the right, evidence of former human habitation. At 1.1 miles, a collapsed chimney on the left marks a former house site. Soon after on the right, you'll see a rock wall and, beyond, a collapsed log cabin. The trail passes more rock piles and rock walls. At 1.2 miles, you'll pass the end of a rock wall, soon rockhopping a small creek and curving up right to pass more rock walls.

A ruined cabin stands off to the right; you'll then drop to ford the Hughes River and walk up to a junction with the Nicholson Hollow Trail in front of Corbin Cabin at 1.4 miles. (To the left, the Nicholson Hollow Trail descends along the Hughes River into Nicholson Hollow, passes junctions with the Hannah Run and Hot Mountain–Short Mountain Trails, and emerges from the park to join the Weakley Hollow Fire Road in 4.0 miles from Corbin Cabin.) To complete this loop back to Skyline Drive, turn right on the Nicholson Hollow Trail at Corbin Cabin.

Heading upstream along the Hughes River, you'll walk up to a junction at 1.6 miles. (To the left, the Indian Run Trail connects this upper end of the Nicholson Hollow Trail with the Corbin Mountain Trail in 1.7 miles, with access then to Old Rag Fire Road to the west; the Corbin Mountain Trail circles east to connect with the lower part of the Nicholson Hollow Trail; these trails offer opportunities for several longer backcountry hikes.) For this hike, continue straight up the Nicholson Hollow Trail.

The trail follows an old road through here. Ford Indian Run, a tributary of the Hughes River, at 1.7 miles. Watch for a large oak on the right at 2.0 miles. The trail then follows a creek on the left to begin a steep, rocky climb up the ridge. You'll pass a spring at 2.8 miles. After more steep uphill hiking, emerge on Skyline Drive at 3.2 miles. Turn left, walking along the drive for 100 yards to cross and pick up an old roadway on the west side of the drive. Walking into the woods, you'll reach a junction at 3.3 miles (the Crusher Ridge Trail is to the right); bear left to reach the AT at 3.4 miles. Now turn right to head back to the beginning of the loop.

The AT leads uphill, curving right over a ridge and reaching an intersection with the Crusher Ridge Trail at 3.6 miles. (To the right, the trail descends to the previous junction; to the left, the Crusher Ridge Trail heads out along Crusher Ridge, eventually descending to the park boundary where it dead-ends in 1.7 miles.) Continue straight on the AT.

The trail switchbacks downhill, rises, and then drops again to reach the side trail to the right at 4.2 miles that leads to the parking area where you began the hike.

28 | PASSAMAQUODDY TRAIL

**Distance: 1.8 miles one-way; Lower Little Stony Man,
    0.5 mile one-way**
Difficulty: Moderate
Elevation gain: 500 feet
Cautions: Rocky
Connections: AT, Skyland Road, Bushytop Trail

Attractions: This route gives quick access to the lower ledge of Little Stony Man and forms a good loop hike with the Appalachian Trail (AT). Passamaquoddy is an Indian word meaning "abounding in pollock"; the trail was built by George Freeman Pollock for his guests at Skyland, and named to honor his parents.

Trailhead: At Mile 39.1, pull into the parking area on the right, which gives access to the AT.

Description: From the parking area, head up the rocky trail into the woods to a junction with the Appalachian Trail in 50 yards; turn left to head south on the AT. The trail curves left and passes beside Skyline Drive, high above the roadway. At 0.3 mile, switchback right and ascend to a junction at 0.4 mile with the Passamaquoddy Trail (to the left, the AT ascends to Little Stony Man Cliffs in another 0.2 mile); stay straight on the Passamaquoddy.

At 0.5 mile you emerge on the lower ledge of the Little Stony Man Cliffs, with good views of the valley from the bare rock bluff. The trail passes below the upper cliff of Little Stony Man and then penetrates a hemlock wood to pass under a powerline at 1.3 miles and reach Furnace Spring on the left. A copper smelter was located here that handled the ore once mined on Stony Man Mountain. Now the spring supplies water for Skyland. You'll see water emerging below the trail.

Just beyond the spring, you reach a junction at 1.4 miles with the old Skyland Road, which gave access to the Skyland Resort before the park was established (to the right, the road descends the mountain and emerges from the park as VA 672, but there is no public access); turn left up the road.

Soon you reach another junction (to the left, you can pick up a horse trail that leads to the Stony Man Nature Trail parking area and can be used for a loop hike with the AT, returning to the parking area on Skyline Drive where you started—see hike 29). To complete the Passamaquoddy Trail, stay straight up the road.

You'll pass a steep service road on the left that dead-ends up the slope. Stay straight on Skyland Road. At 1.5 miles, the road continues into the Skyland cabin area, and the Passamaquoddy Trail turns left off the road on a footpath; turn left up the trail.

Pass behind the Skyland amphitheater and at 1.6 miles emerge on a paved road that leads left toward the north entrance of Skyland; the cabin area is to the right. The trail crosses the road and continues up through the woods to a junction at 1.7 miles (a paved path on the right leads down from the resort dining room to the cabin area); turn left up the paved path.

As the path swings right, a side path left leads to an employee area. Just below the dining room at 1.8 miles, the trail turns off the paved path to follow a graveled path that passes below the lodge office, eventually connecting with the paved road on the other side of the complex at 2.0 miles. (Across the road, you can pick up the Bushytop Trail to Millers Head, hike 32.)

Thorofare Mountain Overlook of Old Rag from Skyline Drive, south of Passamaquoddy Trail

THE SKYLAND AREA

Skyland has grown from George Pollock's mountain retreat. Newer buildings house the restaurant/gift shop and registration. Visitor accommodations are in lodge buildings and small cabins on a lower shoulder of the mountain, where Pollock's camp was located. Several of the old cabins still exist, including Massanutten Lodge, the 1911 home of Addie Nairn, who later married Pollock. The only original cabin in which visitors can stay is Byrds Nest, the cabin of Governor and Senator Harry F. Byrd Sr., a park supporter; the cabin had belonged to his father. Several trails offer interesting hikes out of the Skyland area.

Skyline Drive: The North Entrance to the Skyland Resort is on the right at Mile 41.7. The road passes a parking area on the right for the Stony Man

Massanutten Lodge

Map 4. The Skyland Area

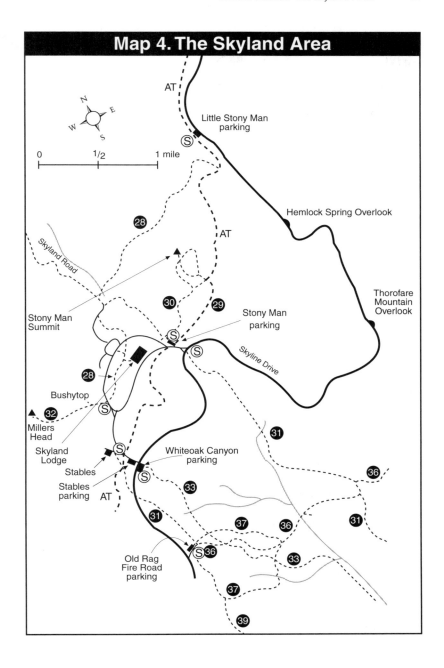

Nature Trail (hike 29) and two horse trails (hikes 30 and 31), then continues on to pass the lodge dining hall to the left and enters the cabin area. Continuing along Skyline Drive, the South Entrance to the resort is at Mile 42.5. Turning here, you pass the lodge area to the right and enter the cabin area to access the trail to Millers Head (hike 32).

29 STONY MAN NATURE TRAIL/ LITTLE STONY MAN CLIFFS

Distance: 1.6 miles one-way; Stony Man summit, 0.7 mile one-way
Difficulty: Moderate
Elevation change: 400 feet
Cautions: Steep ascent, rocky
Connections: AT, Stony Man Horse Trail

Attractions: The nature trail takes you to the summit of Stony Man Mountain for panoramic views, and a side trip on the AT takes you to the cliffs of Little Stony Man. The nature trail has numbered posts corresponding to a nature trail brochure that is available wherever books are sold in the park. The Stony Man summit is the second-highest peak in the park, at 4,011 feet.

Trailhead: At Mile 41.7 turn right into the North Entrance to Skyland, and immediately turn right into trailhead parking for the nature trail. The Appalachian Trail from the south crosses the island between the South and North Entrances to Skyland and enters the Stony Man parking area, picking up the nature trail.

Description: Head up the

Stony Man

paved path at the right corner of the parking area, and then bear to the right on the graveled path. Begin an ascent through blooming pinxter-flower at the end of May and early June. At 0.2 mile, a bench sits on the right. Then at 0.4 mile there is a junction. (To the left lies a connector to the Stony Man Horse Trail, hike 30; the Appalachian Trail (AT), which has been following the nature trail, here turns off to the right, which is the route to the cliffs of Little Stony Man—at this junction on Stony Man Mountain, the AT is at its highest point in the park.) To reach the summit of Stony Man, continue straight up the mountain.

At 0.5 mile there is a fork for a short loop over the summit; stay right. You'll pass a view to the right of distant Nicholson Hollow on the east side of the ridge. The trail passes an old copper mine site on the left and reaches the summit at a four-way intersection at 0.7 mile. (To the left is the return part of the summit loop; straight ahead is the Stony Man Horse Trail, hike 30.) Turn right to get to the summit view in 70 yards, where you'll stand on bare rock to look westward to Shenandoah Valley. You are standing at the top of Stony Man's forehead, the profile visible from the Stony Man Overlook at Mile 38.6.

Retrace your steps to the four-way intersection (Stony Man Horse Trail, hike 30, is now to your right, and the way you came up is to your left); go straight ahead to descend on the return portion of the summit loop and close the loop at the fork, from where you stay right to descend to the junction with the AT at a total of 1.0 mile (to the right is the connector to the Stony Man Horse Trail, hike 30); if you're just out for a walk to the summit, stay straight to return to the parking area at 1.4 miles; to get to Little Stony Man, turn left on the AT, headed north.

The trail descends, emerging on the cliffs of Little Stony Man at 1.6 miles. If you look carefully below, you'll see the lower ledge of Little Stony Man Cliffs, traversed by the Passamaquoddy Trail (hike 28).

(You can continue on the AT, descending steeply with switchbacks, to a junction at 1.8 miles with the Passamaquoddy Trail to the left. If you continue to the right on the AT, in another 0.4 mile you reach the Little Stony Man parking area on Skyline Drive at Mile 39.1. You can also walk a loop by turning left on the Passamaquoddy Trail and following it to where the trail emerges on Skyland Road for a total of 3.0 miles—see hike 28; then turn left up to a junction where you turn left on a side road that's open to horses. The side road becomes a trail, passing under a powerline and turning right steeply up the slope. At 3.8 miles, you reach the Stony Man Horse Trail, hike 30. To the right the trail leads out to the North Entrance road in 50 yards; to the left the horse trail continues to the summit of Stony Man; turn left on the horse trail and soon turn off to the right to reach the nature trailhead parking on the right to complete the loop.)

30 | STONY MAN HORSE TRAIL

Distance: 0.7 mile one-way
Difficulty: Moderate
Elevation gain: 400 feet
Cautions: Steep ascent, rocky
Connections: Stony Man Nature Trail, Skyland Road,
    Skyland–Big Meadows Horse Trail

Attractions: This trail provides another route to the summit of Stony Man Mountain. There is no horse trail connection on the summit of Stony Man, so if you are on horses, you must ride back down the mountain the way you came.

View from Stony Man

Trailhead: At Mile 41.7 turn right into the North Entrance to Skyland, and immediately turn right into trailhead parking for the nature trail. At the far left end of the parking area, a path leads into the woods a few yards to access the Stony Man Horse Trail to the right. (To the left, the trail reaches the connector horse trail on the right in a short distance that leads to the Skyland Road; see hikes 28 and 29. A little farther on, in 70 yards, the trail emerges on the paved road. This parking area also provides access to the Skyland–Big Meadows Horse Trail, hike 31; walk or ride to the North Entrance and cross Skyline Drive to the trailhead on the east. The Stony Man parking area is frequently used for loading and unloading horses because of this easy access to horse trails.)

Description: Turn right on the Stony Man Horse Trail and begin a steep, rocky ascent of Stony Man Mountain. At 0.2 mile, the trail forks (to the right is hiker-only access to Stony Man Nature Trail, hike 29, in 100 yards); take the left fork to continue up toward the summit of Stony Man.

Ascend to a bare rock overlook at 0.5 mile, with Skyland laid out to the left and a view to the right across the valley. Then at 0.6 mile, the horse trail ends at a four-way junction (Stony Man Nature Trail, hike 29, is a loop both straight ahead and to the right); turn left to reach the summit—horses cannot be ridden to the summit; hitching rails are provided for horses here.

Walk 70 yards to the summit of bare rock with a view westward to Shenandoah Valley. You are standing at the top of Stony Man's forehead.

31 | SKYLAND–BIG MEADOWS HORSE TRAIL

Distance: 11.3 miles one-way
Difficulty: Moderate
Elevation change: 1,100 feet
Cautions: Skyline Drive crossings, narrow and rocky in places
Connections: Stony Man Horse Trail, Old Rag Fire Road, Limberlost Trail, Whiteoak Canyon Trail, Whiteoak Fire Road, Cedar Run Trail, Rose River Loop, Rose River Fire Road, Story-of-the-Forest Nature Trail, Tanners Ridge Horse Trail

Attractions: This trail leaves Skyland for a long trek south to Big Meadows. Where the trail crosses Whiteoak Run, you can walk a short distance down the Whiteoak Canyon Trail (hike 33) for views of the upper falls of Whiteoak Run. Later the trail passes below Hawksbill Mountain, the highest peak in the park, and crosses the Rose River Fire Road before ending at Big Meadows at the Tanners Ridge parking area.

Trailhead: At Mile 41.7 turn right into the North Entrance to Skyland, and immediately turn right into trailhead parking for Stony Man Horse Trail and Nature Trail. Walk or ride east along the side of the road 0.1 mile to Skyline Drive. Cross the drive and pick up the Skyland–Big Meadows Horse Trail on the east side. Concrete posts along the trail mark miles and half miles.

(An alternative starting point is the stables area at the Skyland South Entrance; from Skyline Drive, turn right at Mile 42.5; in a short distance, at a fork in the road, turn left to the stables.)

Description: Across from the Stony Man parking area, the trail descends east from Skyline Drive, crossing the upper reaches of Whiteoak Run at 0.6 mile and connecting with the Old Rag Fire Road (hike 36) at 1.2 miles. Turn right on the road and then watch for the trail to turn off left back into the woods in a short distance.

(From the stable area at the Skyland South Entrance, the trail crosses to the east side of Skyline Drive. After a little downhill, you'll pass through old apple and cherry orchards with deer browsing beneath the trees and grouse scurrying out of the way. At 0.4 mile, the trail crosses the upper end of the Limberlost Trail, hike 37, and reaches a junction with the Old Rag Fire Road, hike 36. To the right is a parking area that lies just off Skyline Drive at Mile 43.0; turn left on Old Rag Fire Road. Cross the Whiteoak Canyon Trail, hike 33, and continue down the road to enter "The Limberlost" hemlock forest. At 0.9 mile, cross the lower section of the Limberlost Trail. The road soon descends to cross the upper stream of Whiteoak Run. At 1.5 miles is a junction; the fire road continues straight toward Old Rag Mountain, and just up the road is where the northern access for the Skyland–Big Meadows Horse Trail joins the road from the left; the horse trail turns to the right off the road—the two access routes meet here.)

Now follow a graveled path through the woods. Watch for a large snag on the right and a huge oak, and then large hemlocks at 2.0 miles. At 2.5 miles, descend steeply to cross the Whiteoak Canyon Trail at 3.0 miles. Just to the right are hitching rails, where you can leave horses; walk down the hiking trail to the left for 0.1 mile to a high overlook of the upper falls of Whiteoak Run. From the hitching rails, continue right to a ford of Whiteoak Run. This is the lowest point on the trail; from here you'll ascend toward Big Meadows. On the other side of Whiteoak Run, pick up the Whiteoak Fire Road and ascend.

At 4.7 miles is a junction (straight ahead, Whiteoak Fire Road emerges in 0.1 mile on Skyline Drive at Mile 45.0); to continue toward Big Meadows, turn left on a narrow and rocky trail. Watch for stinging nettle.

At 5.2 miles, there is another junction (the Cedar Run Trail, hike 40, to the right leads 50 yards up to Hawksbill Gap on Skyline Drive at Mile 45.6); stay straight on the horse trail.

At 6.6 miles, a side trail on the right leads out to the Upper Hawksbill parking on Skyline Drive at Mile 46.7; bear left to continue south on the horse trail.

The trail circles east below Spitler Hill and then curves south at 7.0 miles to make a steep, winding descent before curving back west at 7.6 miles. The trail parallels the cove of the Rose River, finally crossing two branches forming the headwaters of the river at 8.6 miles. At 9.1 miles the Rose River Loop (hike 43) joins the horse trail, coming in from the left; go straight, where the two routes coincide to a junction with the Rose River Fire Road at 9.6 miles (the road leads right to Skyline Drive at Fishers Gap at Mile 49.4; to the left is hike 44); the horse trail crosses Rose River Fire Road, angled to the left. Continuing through the forest, the trail rises to cross Skyline Drive to the west side at 9.7 miles.

The trail parallels Skyline Drive on the west, eventually entering the Big Meadows area and crossing the Story-of-the-Forest Nature Trail (hike 46) at 11.0 miles. At 11.2 miles is a junction (to the left lies a maintenance area that has a corral, but it's no longer open to the public); turn right for 0.1 mile to reach a side trail left to parking for the Tanners Ridge Horse Trail (hike 49), which continues straight from the junction. This parking area is frequently used for loading and unloading horses.

32 | BUSHYTOP/MILLERS HEAD TRAIL

**Distance: 0.8 mile one-way; Bushytop Overlook,
    0.2 mile one-way**
Difficulty: Moderate
Elevation loss: 300 feet
Cautions: Rocky in places
Connections: Passamaquoddy Trail

Attractions: This short walk takes you over Bushytop Mountain and out to Millers Head. These two lower peaks on the west side of the Blue Ridge offer grand views of Kettle Canyon in the side of the mountain from Bushytop and of Shenandoah Valley from Millers Head. This is a favorite hike for those staying at Skyland, especially at sunset, but return before it gets totally dark, or bring a flashlight.

Trailhead: Turn right into the South Entrance to Skyland at Mile 42.5. Pass the stables on the left, where you can take guided horse rides; the Appalachian Trail (AT) crosses the road near the stables. Where a right turn leads to the restaurant/registration area, continue straight. You'll soon descend into the lodging complex. The trail to Bushytop and Millers Head begins on the left, across from the Franklin and Winchester lodges; look for a trail post. (If you are not staying at Skyland, you'll need to look for parking in this vicinity.) On the right, among the lodge buildings, the Passamaquoddy Trail (hike 28) leads up past the Skyland Restaurant.

Description: The Bushytop/Millers Head Trail first skirts a service road and then wends its way uphill to a communications installation with large receiving dishes at the top of Bushytop Mountain. Continue straight to reach a junction at 0.2 mile (the trail to Millers Head is to the left); go straight ahead.

In a short way, Bushytop Overlook gives a view of Kettle Canyon below and Skyland back to your right. Return to the junction and turn toward Millers Head.

Descend along the ridgeline with several switchbacks right and left. The trail zigzags down a rock outcrop at 0.7 mile and then winds up to a stone observation deck at the point of Millers Head at 0.8 mile. The view is more than 180 degrees of Page Valley/Shenandoah Valley to the west with Massanutten Mountain in the distance.

SKYLAND TO BIG MEADOWS

The section from Skyland to Big Meadows has some of the most interesting terrain in the park, including numerous waterfalls down Whiteoak and Cedar Runs and Rose River, the highest peak in the park—Hawksbill— and, to the east, Old Rag Mountain, whose bare rock summit looks ragged. Lodges at Skyland and Big Meadows, in addition to the picnic area, wayside, and campground at Big Meadows, provide all services.

Skyline Drive: Just south of the South Entrance to Skyland, Whiteoak Canyon parking lies on the left side of Skyline Drive at Mile 42.6; here you can access the popular Whiteoak Canyon Trail (hike 33) and the numerous waterfalls on Whiteoak Run. South of Whiteoak Canyon parking, you'll reach Old Rag Fire Road (hike 36) on the left at Mile 43.0, which leads east to Old Rag Mountain. Old Rag can also be reached along trails accessed from outside the park on Berry Hollow Fire Road (hike 34) and Weakley Hollow Fire Road (hike 35). The parking area on Old Rag Fire Road, just down from Skyline Drive, is also the trailhead for the Limberlost Trail (hike 37).

Just south of the Old Rag Fire Road, Skyline Drive passes through an old apple orchard, laden with blooms in early spring and fruit later on. At the Timber Hollow Overlook on the right at Mile 43.3, you'll see Hawksbill Mountain to the left, the highest peak in the park, and Nakedtop Mountain. In the foreground to the left lies Timber Hollow, which is actually the upper end of Bruacker Hollow. The prominent peak to the right is Pollock Knob, named in 1951 in honor of George F. Pollock, the founder of Skyland Resort who helped lead the effort to establish Shenandoah National Park. By descending steps from this overlook into the clearing below, you can connect with the Appalachian Trail (AT), which runs below the overlook.

You'll reach the Crescent Rock Overlook at Mile 44.4, with views west from Crescent Rock and Bettys Rock (hike 38). Across the drive from the overlook lies the trailhead for the Crescent Rock Trail (hike 39).

Whiteoak Fire Road is on the left side of Skyline Drive at Mile 45.0, where there's room for a couple of cars to park. (At 0.1 mile down this road, you can connect with the Skyland–Big Meadows Horse Trail, hike 31, which follows the fire road to the left to reach the upper falls of Whiteoak Canyon in 1.7 miles; this is the shortest access to the falls.)

Hawksbill Gap lies at Mile 45.6 on Skyline Drive, where you can access the Cedar Run Trail (hike 40) on the left and the Hawksbill Trail (hike 41) on the right. Old Rag View Overlook on the left at Mile 46.5 offers another look at Old Rag Mountain. Upper Hawksbill parking lies on the right at

Map 5. Skyland to Big Meadows

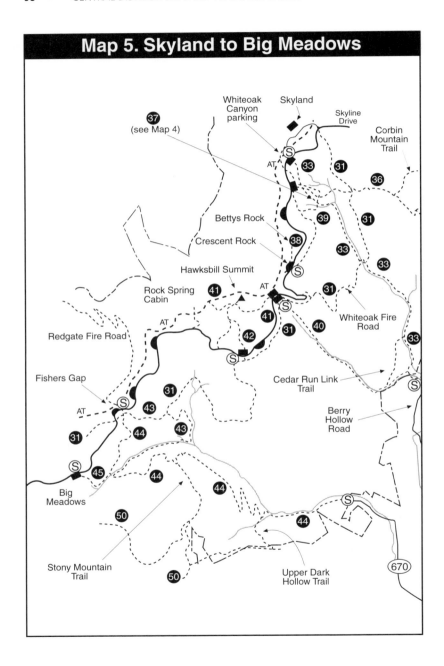

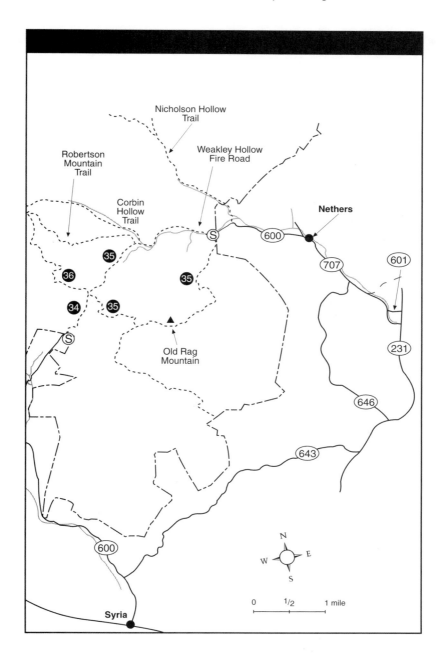

Mile 46.7, where the Hawksbill Mountain Trail (hike 42) leads to the mountain's summit.

Continuing south on Skyline Drive, on the right at Mile 47.1 is the service road that ascends to Byrds Nest No. 2 shelter. You'll pass another service road on the right at Mile 47.8, which leads to the Potomac Appalachian Trail Club's Rock Spring Cabin; the Rock Spring Hut on the Appalachian Trail (AT) stands near the cabin. On the right at Mile 48.1 is Spitler Knoll Overlook; a 50-yard path at the north end of the overlook parking leads steeply down to the AT, where you can turn right to walk to Rock Spring Cabin in 0.8 mile. From the overlook, named for a family that had a farm nearby, you'll see Blackrock Mountain to the left where the lodge and campground near Big Meadows are located; to the right stands Nakedtop.

At Mile 49.0 on the right, at Franklin Cliffs Overlook, named for William B. Franklin, a Union general in the Civil War, you can see the town of Stanley below and the high peak of Blackrock to your left.

Fishers Gap Overlook lies at Mile 49.4 on the right side of Skyline Drive; Rose River Fire Road (hikes 43 and 44) begins on the left side of the drive to head east down the mountain. The Skyland–Big Meadows Horse Trail (hike 31) crosses the drive at Mile 49.5. Beyond you'll enter Big Meadows.

Trailheads located outside the park: Several of the trailheads in this section are reached not via Skyline Drive but by side roads entering the park from the east. To take hikes 34, 35, or 44, exit Skyline Drive at Mile 31.5 to the north, in Thornton Gap. Then descend east on US 211. Turn south on US 522 in Sperryville, then south again on VA 231 to reach trailhead parking on Berry Hollow Fire Road and Weakley Hollow Fire Road.

33 | WHITEOAK CANYON TRAIL

Distance: 5.3 miles one-way; Upper Falls,
2.6 miles one-way
Difficulty: Moderate
Elevation loss: 2,350 feet
Cautions: Rocky, steep descent
Connections: Limberlost Trail, Old Rag Fire Road, Skyland–
Big Meadows Horse Trail, Whiteoak Fire Road, Cedar Run
Link Trail, Cedar Run Trail

Attractions: This trail gives access to the park's largest collection of waterfalls in one of the deepest canyons. The long cascade of the upper falls is especially scenic, but the others should not be missed either. As you

Upper Falls on Whiteoak Run

descend into Whiteoak Canyon, the creek cascades into pools among large hemlocks, while the trail heads down amid blooming laurel in May and June.

Trailhead: Turn in at Whiteoak Canyon parking on the left side of Skyline Drive at Mile 42.6. This is the upper trailhead.

To reach the lower trailhead, from Thornton Gap take US 211 east; turn south on US 522 in Sperryville. In 0.6 mile turn right onto VA 231. At 11.0 miles, turn right on VA 643. At 15.5 miles, you'll reach a junction with VA 600 (to the left is the community of Syria on VA 670); turn to the right up VA 600 toward the park. At 19.3 miles, the road crosses Cedar Run and reaches parking on the left. If you enter the park on this end, the Park Service now collects an access fee, but your Skyline Drive park pass is good for this fee. From the lower trailhead, follow the trail description in reverse.

Description: From the upper trailhead, the trail enters the woods and descends. At 0.5 mile, you'll cross a branch of Whiteoak Run on a footbridge. Soon after, the trail crosses a leg of the Limberlost Trail loop (hike 37)—stay straight—and at 0.6 mile crosses Old Rag Fire Road (hike 36)—again, stay straight. At 0.8 mile, cross the other side of the Limberlost Trail (stay straight) as the trail bears left along another branch of Whiteoak Run on your right. The trail crosses a large bridge over this branch of Whiteoak Run at 1.2 miles and then follows the main stem of Whiteoak Run downstream on your left.

At 1.5 miles descend more steeply. The trail passes through large blocks of stone and at 2.4 miles turns left to cross a bridge over Whiteoak Run. A makeshift path straight along the creek connects with the Whiteoak Fire Road. After crossing the bridge, turn to the right downstream. Soon on your right you'll see a ford across to the Whiteoak Fire Road. You'll pass hitching rails and reach the Skyland–Big Meadows Horse Trail (hike 31) up to the left; stay straight.

At 2.5 miles a path on the right leads to a view above the upper Whiteoak Falls. At 2.6 miles another path leads out onto rocks for a bird's-eye view of the 86-foot-high falls, the second highest in the park. The trail then begins a steep descent of rock steps to a junction at 2.8 miles (a 100-yard side trail to the right leads to the base of the upper falls); stay straight.

Continuing, you'll step down cemented stone steps and stone slabs. At 2.9 miles the trail swings around a huge boulder above a cascade in the creek. The trail then descends left and right to a view of another falls of Whiteoak Run at 3.1 miles. Continue to descend, reaching an overlook of a third falls at 3.2 miles. As you continue the descent, watch for large hemlocks and poplars. At 3.3 miles you'll pass a short falls.

The trail then reaches an overlook of another falls at 3.4 miles. Descending past this falls, you'll see a path to the right that leads down to a pool in the creek. The trail switchbacks down through rocks and wild hydrangea shrubs to emerge at the sixth and last falls of Whiteoak Run at

4.0 miles. This is a two-step falls; you'll see the second below.

Once below the falls, the descent is not so steep. Rockhop a side stream. Whiteoak Run descends in small cascades. You'll pass a little pool below a cascade in the creek.

At 4.5 miles is a junction. (The Cedar Run Link Trail to the right links with the Cedar Run Trail, hike 40, for one of the best loop hikes in the park: along the link trail to the Cedar Run Trail, up Cedar Run to Hawksbill Gap on Skyline Drive at Mile 45.6, north on the Skyland–Big Meadows Horse Trail, hike 31, and right on the Whiteoak Fire Road to rejoin the Whiteoak Canyon Trail above the upper falls for a loop of 7.8 miles, plus 4.8 miles round-trip from the parking area.) Stay straight ahead past the Cedar Run Link Trail.

Continue your descent along Whiteoak Run, crossing the creek on a metal bridge and reaching a junction at 5.1 miles (the Cedar Run Trail, hike 40, is to the right); bear left on the Whiteoak Canyon Trail.

Ford Cedar Run; a bridge here was damaged in a 1996 storm. You'll reach the upper end of the parking area for the lower trailhead at 5.3 miles. Walk through the parking area to cross back over Cedar Run and pass through more parking to reach VA 600 (Berry Hollow Fire Road).

34 BERRY HOLLOW FIRE ROAD AND SADDLE TRAIL TO OLD RAG

Distance: 2.8 miles one-way
Difficulty: Moderate
Elevation gain: 1,700 feet
Cautions: Uphill, rocky and rutted
Connections: Whiteoak Canyon Trail, Cedar Run Trail, Old Rag Fire Road, Weakley Hollow Fire Road, Ridge Trail

Attractions: The rock boulders of Old Rag's summit offer grand views in all directions. Clouds foam up from below to sometimes obscure the view, creating a surreal scene of bare rock and billowing mist. From a distance on a clear day, the bare granite on top of Old Rag makes the peak look ragged, which is how it got its name. This is an easier hike to the summit of Old Rag Mountain than the Ridge Trail (hike 35), and it's shorter than the Old Rag Fire Road from Skyline Drive (hike 36). Berry Hollow Fire Road also gives access to the lower end of the Whiteoak Canyon and Cedar Run Trails.

Trailhead: This trailhead is reached not from Skyline Drive, but by side roads entering the park from the east. From Thornton Gap to the north, take US 211 east; turn south on US 522 in Sperryville. In 0.6 mile turn right

Rocky summit of Old Rag

onto VA 231. At 11.0 miles, turn right on VA 643. At 15.5 miles, you'll reach a junction with VA 600 (to the left, you can reach the community of Syria, located on VA 670); turn to the right up VA 600 toward the park. At 19.3 miles, the road crosses Cedar Run and passes parking on the left for the lower end of the Cedar Run and Whiteoak Canyon Trails. The road crosses Whiteoak Run. Continue up the narrow gravel road to its end at 20.2 miles. Berry Hollow Fire Road heads uphill to the right. Here the park now collects an access fee; your park pass is good for this fee.

Description: The old road winds uphill, often rocky and rutted from erosion. You'll reach a junction at 0.8 mile; the post office/store for the community of Old Rag once stood here. (From the junction, Old Rag Fire Road, hike 36, heads west to Skyline Drive in 5.0 miles; just up that road and to the right, the Weakley Hollow Fire Road, hike 35, leads down to trailhead parking for Old Rag on the north.) Turn right on the Saddle Trail to ascend toward the summit of Old Rag.

You'll ascend along an old roadway to the Old Rag Shelter at 1.2 miles; the shelter is no longer used for overnight camping. No camping is allowed on Old Rag above 2,800 feet because so many people hike to the top of the mountain.

The trail passes through a forest of large trees, making some switch-backs, to reach Byrds Nest No. 1 shelter at 2.3 miles, also a day-use-only structure. From the shelter, the trail ascends stone steps and switchbacks and passes through boulders to the top of Old Rag at 2.8 miles. (On Old Rag, the Saddle Trail ends where the Ridge Trail begins a rough descent 2.6 miles to the Weakley Hollow Fire Road, hike 35. You must be strong and agile to make this descent; do not go this way on rainy days when the rocks are wet and slippery.)

35   RIDGE TRAIL, SADDLE TRAIL, AND WEAKLEY HOLLOW FIRE ROAD OVER OLD RAG

Distance: 7.1-mile loop; Old Rag Summit, 2.6 miles one-way
Difficulty: Strenuous
Elevation change: 2,284 feet
Cautions: Rock scramble, not recommended when rocks are wet; lots of people on weekends and holidays
Connections: Nicholson Hollow Trail, Old Rag Fire Road, Berry Hollow Fire Road, Robertson Mountain Trail, Corbin Hollow Trail

Attractions: This rough but rewarding hike takes you over the summit of Old Rag Mountain for panoramic views from the bare rock peak. Although the climb to the top is fun, it is also difficult and should be attempted only by experienced hikers. Because of the popularity of this hike, try going on a weekday when fewer people are about. In spring, watch for blooming mountain laurel, pinxter-flower, hydrangea, and maple-leaf viburnum.

Trailhead: This trailhead is reached not from Skyline Drive but by side roads entering the park from the east. From Thornton Gap to the north, take US 211 east; at Sperryville, turn southeast on US 522 for 0.6 mile to a right turn onto VA 231. At 8.7 miles, turn right onto VA 601 and then at 9.1

miles turn right to continue on VA 601. The road bears right at 10.0 miles and becomes VA 707. Stay left at 11.7 miles as the road becomes VA 600 in the community of Nethers. At 12.2 miles you'll reach lower parking for the trailhead; on busy weekends and holidays, parking is restricted to this lower lot, which will add 0.9 mile one-way to your hike. At 12.8 miles, you'll pass the end of the Nicholson Hollow Trail on the right, which descends 5.8 miles from Skyline Drive. You reach the upper trailhead parking for Old Rag at 13.1 miles. The park provides information and collects an access fee here at a kiosk; your park pass is good for this fee. The kiosk is staffed from Memorial Day through the last weekend in October.

Description: The Weakley Hollow Fire Road, which heads straight into the woods, is your return route; take the Ridge Trail to the left to hike the loop clockwise. Ascend through hemlock on a broad path. The trail switchbacks up the slope of Old Rag.

At 1.6 miles, you'll reach the bare rock and boulders that make up the top of the mountain. From here it is a long and difficult rock scramble up to the peak; keep an eye on the blue blazes to find your way.

At 1.8 miles, drop into a narrow lava dike where softer rock has eroded from between granite walls; the trail turns left at the end of the dike. You'll then drop through a saddle and continue up the mountain.

The trail penetrates a rock squeeze and at 1.9 miles passes under a leaning boulder. Then turn to the right to the opening of another eroded dike, and turn left inside. Out the other end, turn right. You'll have a brief reprieve before continuing the rock scramble. At one point, you must belly-up a boulder.

At 2.6 miles you reach the 3,268-foot summit of Old Rag. A little farther, you can scramble up rocks on the right to pause for a sweeping view; take care. At the summit, the Ridge Trail ends; but the path continues on

Eroded dike on Old Rag

as the Saddle Trail. Descend through boulders, switchbacks, and stone steps to reach Byrds Nest No. 1 shelter at 3.1 miles. Built in 1961, the shelter is day-use only; there is no camping on Old Rag above 2,800 feet. A fire road on the left heads southeast to end at the park boundary.

The trail bears right past the shelter, continuing to descend with switchbacks and through a rock passage. A large tree arched over the trail introduces an area of large trees. The Old Rag Shelter stands at 4.2 miles; the shelter is also day-use only. The trail turns right on an old roadway. At 4.6 miles, there is a junction of roads (to the left, the Berry Hollow Fire Road, hike 34, leads down to the park boundary and trailhead parking in 0.8 mile; this provides an easier route up Old Rag); turn right on the Old Rag Fire Road. Shortly, there is another junction (Old Rag Fire Road continues on to the left to reach Skyline Drive in 5.0 miles); turn right again, now on the Weakley Hollow Fire Road.

At 5.7 miles you'll pass the Robertson Mountain Trail on the left and at 5.8 miles the Corbin Hollow Trail, also on the left; at both junctions, stay straight. Watch for designated campsites to be established along this section. The road crosses Brokenback Run on a metal bridge and follows the creek downstream. At 7.0 miles, bear right to ford the creek to a series of metal and wooden bridges that take you over branches of the creek. After you cross a side stream on a bridge, you emerge back at trailhead parking at 7.1 miles.

36 | OLD RAG FIRE ROAD

Distance: 5.0 miles one-way
Difficulty: Moderate
Elevation loss: 1,460 feet
Cautions: Steep ascent to summit of Old Rag from end of
fire road
Connections: Skyland–Big Meadows Horse Trail, Limberlost
Trail, Whiteoak Canyon Trail, Corbin Mountain Trail,
Corbin Hollow Trail, Robertson Mountain Trail, Saddle
Trail, Weakley Hollow Fire Road, Berry Hollow Fire Road

Attractions: This old road passes through a forest of hemlocks called "The Limberlost" and provides access from Skyline Drive to Old Rag Mountain.

Trailhead: At Mile 43.0, turn in at Old Rag Fire Road on the left side of Skyline Drive—there's no sign. You'll find a parking area that is also the trailhead for the Limberlost Trail on the left.

Description: As you walk down Old Rag Fire Road, the horse trail from the stables at the Skyland South Entrance joins the road on the left (this is a

Old Rag

leg of the Skyland–Big Meadows Horse Trail, hike 31). Soon after, the Whiteoak Canyon Trail (hike 33) for hikers crosses the road (stay straight) and you'll then enter The Limberlost, a forest of 270- to 370-year-old hemlocks. At 0.6 mile, the lower portion of the Limberlost Loop Trail crosses the road (stay straight). (See map 4 for more detail on this upper section.)

The road then descends to cross the upper part of Whiteoak Run. Soon after, you'll reach a fork (to the right, a short side path provides a turnaround area for guided horse rides from the stables); stay with the road to the left as it ascends.

At 1.1 miles is a junction (the Skyland–Big Meadows Horse Trail, hike 31, turns off the road to the right); stay straight. Just up the road is another junction (the Skyland–Big Meadows Horse Trail comes in on the left from the Skyland North Entrance); continue east (right) on Old Rag Fire Road.

At 1.9 miles is a junction (the Corbin Mountain Trail to the left leads off the road up to a junction with the Indian Run Trail, and then over Corbin Mountain to the Nicholson Hollow Trail, hike 27, in 4.4 miles); stay straight.

At 2.4 miles reach another junction (the Corbin Hollow Trail leads left down the hollow of Brokenback Run to connect with the Weakley Hollow Fire Road in 2.0 miles); stay straight. And at 2.5 miles is one more junction (the Robertson Mountain Trail leads left over Robertson Mountain to connect with the Weakley Hollow Fire Road in 2.4 miles); again, stay straight.

The Old Rag Fire Road descends into the gap between the Blue Ridge to the west and Old Rag Mountain to the east, ending at 5.0 miles at a junction.

(The Berry Hollow Fire Road, hike 34, leads straight 0.8 mile down to a parking area at the end of vehicle access from the east. The Weakley Hollow Fire Road, hike 35, comes in on the left; just beyond, the Saddle Trail heads up to the summit of Old Rag Mountain in another 2.0 miles.)

37 | LIMBERLOST TRAIL

Distance: 1.3-mile loop
Difficulty: Easy
Elevation change: Gently sloping
Cautions: No camping
Connections: Old Rag Fire Road, Skyland–Big Meadows
     Horse Trail, Whiteoak Canyon Trail, Crescent Rock Trail

Attractions: The Limberlost Trail wanders through a hemlock forest called "The Limberlost," a name taken by George F. Pollock from the Gene Stratton Porter novel *A Girl of the Limberlost*. The Limberlost, as Porter knew it, was a forested swamp in northeastern Indiana. Addie Nairn, Pollock's wife, purchased this Limberlost of the Blue Ridge to preserve the large hemlocks. The 270- to 370-year-old trees in mornings are shrouded in fog and mist. Deer stand, fearlessly watching. Birds fly among the understory. You may even see a lone black bear climbing a tree. The compact surface of the path and the wooden walkways and bridges make this trail universally accessible as it loops through the forest of large hemlocks.

Trailhead: At Mile 43.0 on Skyline Drive, turn left onto Old Rag Fire Road. In 0.1 mile, you'll find an open area and parking for the trailhead. (Refer to Map 4, The Skyland Area, for details.)

Description: To the left, you'll see the sign for the trailhead where you'll begin the walk. To the right across Old Rag Fire Road lies the return portion of the loop.

In 100 yards after beginning the loop, you'll cross a branch of the Skyland–Big Meadows Horse Trail (hike 31), which leads from the stables near the South Entrance of Skyland to Old Rag Fire Road; continue straight on the Limberlost Trail. The trail passes through mountain laurel, and at 0.3 mile the Whiteoak Canyon Trail (hike 33) crosses the path (stay straight); you'll see the first of several benches that sit along the Limberlost Trail Loop every 400 feet.

The trail curves to the right as it circles in a clockwise direction. At 0.5 mile cross Old Rag Fire Road (stay straight) and, soon after, again cross the Whiteoak Canyon Trail (again stay straight).

At 0.6 mile the trail crosses a bridge over a stream that is part of the headwaters of Whiteoak Run. Watch for huge hemlocks through this next section of trail. At 0.9 mile you'll reach a junction (the Crescent Rock Trail, hike 39, to the left leads 1.1 miles to the Crescent Rock Overlook at Mile 44.4 on Skyline Drive); stay straight.

Cross a long boardwalk over a low, swampy area, where you may see the speckled alder, a large shrub that can get to 20 feet high with broadly elliptical to oval alternating leaves; the shrub is rare in Virginia. At 1.3 miles, emerge to cross Old Rag Fire Road back to the parking area and the trailhead.

38 | CRESCENT ROCK AND BETTYS ROCK

Distance: 100 yards one-way and 0.3 mile one-way
Difficulty: Moderate
Elevation gain: 100 feet to Bettys Rock
Cautions: Steep drop-offs
Connections: AT

Attractions: These two rocks provide panoramic views to the west, with only short walks needed to reach them. Crescent Rock is a popular place

Crescent Rock

for picnics and for viewing sunrises and sunsets. Bettys Rock was likely named for Betty Sours, who once lived in the area.

Trailhead: Turn in at the parking area on the right for the Crescent Rock Overlook at Mile 44.4, where you'll have a view to the southwest of Hawksbill and Nakedtop Mountains. Across the drive you can also access the Crescent Rock Trail (hike 39).

Description: From the south end of the overlook parking, a path leads 100 yards to Crescent Rock, which provides a view west, with Hawksbill Mountain and Nakedtop to the left and Timber/Bruacker Hollow below.

From the north end of the parking area, walk up steps and take the path straight ahead to get to Bettys Rock (a side trail to the left leads 150 yards down to connect with the Appalachian Trail (AT), which passes below Crescent Rock Overlook); stay with the gravel path straight ahead. You'll gradually ascend 0.3 mile to Bettys Rock, another popular place for sunsets with virtually the same view as from Crescent Rock; but also to the right you'll see Millers Head, Bushytop, and Stony Man.

39 | CRESCENT ROCK TRAIL

Distance: 1.1 miles one-way
Difficulty: Easy
Elevation loss: 320 feet
Cautions: None
Connections: Limberlost Trail

Attractions: This trail leads from Crescent Rock Overlook to the Limberlost Trail along a path lined with ferns and frequent pinxter-flower blooming in spring. This trail has been improved somewhat after being eroded by a 1996 storm, but still watch your footing.

Trailhead: From the northern end of the Crescent Rock Overlook parking area on the right at Mile 44.4, cross Skyline Drive to the east side to pick up the Crescent Rock Trail.

Description: Head into the woods. You'll ascend at first and then, after a relatively level section, begin a gradual descent. At 1.0 mile, a path to the left ascends to an old house site with a fence. Then at 1.1 miles, the Crescent Rock Trail ends at the Limberlost Trail (hike 37). (To the left, you can cross a boardwalk and reach trailhead parking for the Limberlost Trail on Old Rag Fire Road in 0.4 mile. To the right, you can reach the Whiteoak Canyon Trail and then Old Rag Fire Road, also in 0.4 mile.)

40 | CEDAR RUN TRAIL

Distance: 3.1 miles one-way
Difficulty: Moderate
Elevation change: 2,100 feet
Cautions: Rocky footing, stinging nettle, steep descent
Connections: Skyland–Big Meadows Horse Trail, Cedar Run
  Link Trail, Whiteoak Canyon Trail

Attractions: Cascading streams make this a wonderful hike through one of the deep canyons of the Blue Ridge. The lower sections of this trail were seriously eroded in a storm in 1996, so use caution as you walk the trail.

Trailhead: At Mile 45.6, Hawksbill Gap has parking on both sides of Skyline Drive. For this hike, park in the small area on the left side of the drive; this is the upper trailhead. To reach the lower trailhead, see Trailhead directions for hike 34, Berry Hollow Fire Road and Saddle Trail to Old Rag.

Description: Take the path straight into the woods. You'll soon encounter a fork (the right fork is the Skyland–Big Meadows Horse Trail headed south toward Big Meadows, hike 31); stay to the left. You'll soon reach another fork (the horse trail turns left toward Skyland to the north); keep straight to continue on the Cedar Run Trail.

Begin a steep, rocky descent along Cedar Run on your right. At 0.6 mile the trail turns right. You'll then pass a number of cascades in the creek and walk along a tall rock wall on the left as the trail continues down Cedar Run Canyon. At 1.1 miles watch for a broad rock beside a nice wading pool in the creek.

At 1.3 miles, the trail bears right to ford Cedar Run below a winding cascade. Ascend from the creek and cross a small side stream. The trail then descends again as Cedar Run continues to cascade steeply down the canyon. After curving left and right, the trail switchbacks down to the creek at 1.6 miles, where you'll see the water gliding down a smooth rock slide. Below is the top of 34-foot Cedar Run Falls. The trail descends steeply to the right to reach a path on the left at 1.7 miles that drops to the bottom of a sluice of water that is the lower part of the falls.

Continuing on the trail, bear left down stone steps. The trail then drops into a forest of large poplars. At 2.2 miles, pass another sluice in the creek as the trail continues steeply down to cross a small side stream. You'll pass another long cascade as you descend through large hemlocks. The trail turns down left, curves right, and turns down left again to ford Cedar Run below a 12-foot waterfall at 2.6 miles.

At 2.8 miles, there's a junction. (The Cedar Run Link Trail to the left links with the Whiteoak Canyon Trail for one of the best loop hikes in the

Cascade on Cedar Run

park: the link trail climbs to circle the ridge separating Cedar Run Canyon from Whiteoak Canyon, passes through a hemlock wood, and curves up Whiteoak Canyon; in 0.8 mile, the trail fords Whiteoak Run and reaches a junction with the Whiteoak Canyon Trail. Turn up Whiteoak Canyon to above the upper falls, hike 33, turn left on the Whiteoak Fire Road, and then turn south on the Skyland–Big Meadows Horse Trail, hike 31, to get back to Hawksbill Gap for a loop hike of 7.8 miles.) Stay straight as the Cedar Run Trail continues steeply down the canyon.

Connect with the Whiteoak Canyon Trail at 3.0 miles (where you can also turn up left to walk the Whiteoak/Cedar Run Loop); bear right on the Whiteoak Canyon Trail and cross Cedar Run on a bridge.

You reach the upper end of the parking area for the trailhead off Berry Hollow Fire Road (hike 34) in 3.1 miles. Walking through the parking area, you'll cross back over Cedar Run and pass through more parking to reach the road.

 41 | **HAWKSBILL TRAIL, SALAMANDER TRAIL, AND AT**

Distance: 2.8-mile loop; Hawksbill Summit, 0.9 mile one-way
Difficulty: Easy
Elevation change: 650 feet
Cautions: Rocky path
Connections: Byrds Nest No. 2 Service Road, Hawksbill Mountain Trail, AT

Attractions: This short hike leads to a grand view atop Hawksbill Mountain, at 4,050 feet the highest peak in Shenandoah National Park; a stone observation platform offers a 360-degree view of the Blue Ridge. As you climb into higher elevations, watch for balsam fir, mountain ash, and, in June and July, the bell-shaped flowers of minnie bush. Also watch for speckled wood lily, sometimes called Clinton's lily, which has small white flowers on a stalk rising from broad basal leaves in May and June. In summer, Allegheny stonecrop grows in rocky areas with pale purplish leaves and clusters of small pink flowers.

Trailhead: Begin at Hawksbill Gap parking, on the right side of Skyline Drive, at Mile 45.6.

Description: The Hawksbill Trail heads straight into the woods to begin ascending as a steep, graveled path. At 0.8 mile, you'll reach a junction with the service road that leads from Skyline Drive at Mile 47.1 to Byrds Nest No. 2; turn right on the road to pass in front of the shelter. Built in 1962, the shelter is for day-use only; there's no camping allowed on the summit of Hawksbill.

On the other side you'll see a path to the right that passes behind the shelter to reconnect with the trail you came up. At 0.9 mile you'll reach the top of Hawksbill Mountain. To the north, look for Stony Man, and to the northeast, Old Rag.

Backtrack down past the shelter to the junction with the Hawksbill Trail at 1.0 mile. Then continue straight down the service road. At 1.1 miles you'll reach a junction. (The service road continues straight to reach Skyline Drive in 0.8 mile, passing in 0.1 mile a left turn onto the Hawksbill

Mountain Trail that leads to the Upper Hawksbill parking area at Mile 46.7 on Skyline Drive.) Turn right on the Salamander Trail, recently renamed from the "Nakedtop" Trail.

You'll pass a rock outcrop with a view to the right while the rocky path bears left along the edge of the mountain. Soon pass a short connector path over to the service road, and then the trail makes a winding descent to a junction with the Appalachian Trail (AT) at 1.8 miles (to the left on the AT lies Fishers Gap in 2.2 miles); turn right to complete the loop.

Along this section of the AT, watch for speckled wood lily and Allegheny stonecrop. The path is rough in places where it traverses talus slopes. The trail then descends into Hawksbill Gap past the parking area to a junction at 2.8 miles (the AT continues straight toward Skyland; the path to the left leads 100 yards down to a spring); take the path on the right, which leads 50 yards back up to the Hawksbill Gap parking area to complete the loop.

Byrds Nest No. 2 (Photo by John Amberson, courtesy of Shenandoah National Park)

42 HAWKSBILL MOUNTAIN TRAIL TO HAWKSBILL SUMMIT

Distance: 1.0 mile one-way
Difficulty: Moderate
Elevation gain: 400 feet
Cautions: Steep ascent
Connections: Skyland–Big Meadows Horse Trail, Byrds Nest
No. 2 Service Road, Salamander Trail, Hawksbill Trail

Attractions: This trail provides access to the summit of Hawksbill Mountain, with less elevation gain than the Hawksbill Trail (hike 41).

Trailhead: Begin at the Upper Hawksbill parking area on the right side of Skyline Drive at Mile 46.7. (Across the road and to the south, you'll also find a short connector to the Skyland–Big Meadows Horse Trail, hike 31.)

Description: From the parking area, head straight into the woods on a graveled path that begins a steep ascent up Hawksbill Mountain. You'll

View from Hawksbill (Photo by John Amberson, courtesy of Shenandoah National Park)

pass benches on the left and the right and, at 0.4 mile, pass a large table rock on the right.

After a level section of trail, you'll reach a junction at 0.7 mile with the Byrds Nest No. 2 Service Road (to the left, the service road descends 0.7 mile to reach Skyline Drive at Mile 47.1; there's very little parking at that location); turn right to reach the summit.

The fire road climbs steeply, entering the no-camping zone around the summit and passing through the standing skeletons of dead trees. You'll reach a junction at 0.8 mile (the Salamander Trail leads left down to the AT); continue up the service road.

At 0.9 mile you'll reach a junction (the Hawksbill Trail is to the right). Just beyond rests the Byrds Nest No. 2 shelter—watch for an abundance of sunflowers in summer. Continue straight in front of the shelter to reach the summit at 1.0 mile, where you'll have views in all directions from the observation platform.

43 | ROSE RIVER LOOP

Distance: 3.9 miles; Rose River Falls, 1.2 miles one-way
Difficulty: Moderate
Elevation change: 800 feet
Cautions: Rocky path, stream crossings and ford
Connections: AT, Skyland–Big Meadows Horse Trail, Rose
    River Fire Road, Dark Hollow Falls Trail

Attractions: Along the Rose River and Hogcamp Branch, you'll pass numerous pools and cascades, including the double drop of Rose River Falls. This is also a good walk for wildflowers in spring. At the north end of the trailhead parking area, a road that crosses Skyline Drive was the Gordonsville Turnpike, which was used during the Civil War by Stonewall Jackson and his troops to cross the mountains on the way east, following their successful Valley Campaign. To the right of Skyline Drive, the road is now called the Redgate Fire Road, and to the left, the Rose River Fire Road. On Hogcamp Branch is a copper mine site that was active in the early 1900s; the mine site was opened originally in 1845–50.

Trailhead: At Mile 49.4, turn to the right into parking for Fishers Gap Overlook, which offers a view down Kite Hollow to the west. To walk the Rose River Loop, cross Skyline Drive to the east and head down the Rose River Fire Road. (At the north end of the parking area is Redgate Fire Road, which accesses the Appalachian Trail (AT), also accessible by a short path at the south end of the overlook. Redgate Fire Road descends the mountain on the west to emerge from the park as VA 611.)

Recreational fishing on the Hogcamp Branch

Description: Very soon after leaving Skyline Drive, the trail turns left off the fire road to make a clockwise loop. This wide path to the left is also part of the Skyland–Big Meadows Horse Trail (hike 31). At 0.1 mile, a post marks 9.5 miles for horse riders from Skyland. At 0.5 mile, you'll reach a junction (the horse trail turns off to the left); continue straight on the Rose River Loop.

At 0.9 mile, the trail bends to the right where an abandoned path leads left. Descend through a hemlock grove to reach the Rose River tumbling into a rock-walled ravine. Bear right to parallel the river downstream. At 1.2 miles, the trail reaches the top of Rose River Falls. A steep path down to the base of the 30-foot drop gives access to the plunge pool, a good swimming hole with clear, cold water even in summer.

Straight ahead, the trail turns up to the right, but there's also a make-shift path to the left that weaves between the rocks and descends steeply to the river below the falls. Turning back left along the stream there, you'll reach the plunge pool of a lower 30-foot falls where the water slides down a crack in the rock to slip into the pool.

Back above the upper falls, turn right on the main trail, which ascends and then bears left to continue following the Rose River downstream. At 1.7 miles, the trail makes a sharp right to begin an ascent up Hogcamp Branch. (A side path to the left at the turn leads onto the point of land between Hogcamp Branch and the Rose River to an old house site.) Heading up Hogcamp Branch, at 1.8 miles you'll pass a concrete block that served as a base for mining machinery at the old copper mine site.

Rockhop a side stream and at 1.9 miles cross Hogcamp Branch on a bridge. Just on the other side, an unmaintained path leads left 0.3 mile up to the Rose River Fire Road—this path is not recommended; stay with the trail to the right and ascend through rocks to continue upstream. You'll pass numerous mini-step cascades, water slides, and pools in this lovely stream. At 2.4 miles, watch for a 15-foot falls.

The trail leads up to a junction with the Rose River Fire Road at 2.9 miles; turn right on the fire road. Cross Hogcamp Branch on a metal bridge below a slender cascade, and reach a junction (the Dark Hollow Falls Trail, hike 45, is to the left; you can reach the bottom of Dark Hollow Falls on Hogcamp Branch in 0.2 mile up this trail); continue straight up the fire road to complete the loop.

At 3.4 miles, a path to the left leads up to the Cave Cemetery. Then just before returning to Skyline Drive, you'll pass the Skyland–Big Meadows Horse Trail (hike 31) turning off the road to the left and close the loop with the horse trail to the right. Up to the drive at 3.9 miles, cross the highway to return to the Fishers Gap Overlook parking.

44 | ROSE RIVER FIRE ROAD

Distance: 6.6 miles one-way
Difficulty: Easy
Elevation gain: 2,000 feet
Cautions: Rocky
Connections: Upper Dark Hollow Trail, Stony Mountain Trail, Rose River Loop, Dark Hollow Falls Trail, Skyland–Big Meadows Horse Trail

Attractions: The Rose River Fire Road into the park was once the Gordonsville Turnpike; Gordonsville lies to the east. Officially, the road was called the "Blue Ridge Turnpike" when Paschal Graves was in charge of construction of the road on the east side of the mountain. When the road was completed in the 1850s, Graves opened an "ordinary," or inn, along the road. His great-great-grandson, Jim Graves, and Jim's wife, Rachel, operate today's Graves' Mountain Lodge, which provides lodging on a working farm. This fire road gives access to the Rose River at its lower end for fishing and swimming, plus access to several trails.

Trailhead: The Rose River Fire Road stretches from Mile 49.4 of Skyline Drive southeast to a parking area just outside the park boundary, near the community of Syria. Since the upper end of the Rose River Fire Road has been described as part of the Rose River Loop (hike 43), this hike will begin at the lower end of the fire road, near Syria, and move toward Skyline Drive.

To reach the lower trailhead, exit the park by taking US 211 east from Thornton Gap. Turn south on US 522 in Sperryville. In 0.6 mile turn right onto VA 231. At 11.0 miles, turn right on VA 643. At 15.5 miles, you'll reach a junction with VA 600; turn left. At 16.4 miles, you'll reach the community of Syria at a junction with VA 670. (You can also reach Syria along VA 670 from VA 231 on the east, passing through Criglersville.) Turn right to continue west on VA 670. You'll pass the Graves' Mountain Lodge on the hill to the left. At 17.8 miles, the road becomes gravel. You'll cross a bridge over the Rose River at 19.0 miles and reach parking at the end of vehicle access at 19.6 miles.

Description: Head up the old road; you'll find the footing rocky. Where the road enters the park, pass around a chain blocking vehicle access. At first, the Rose River lies far below on your right. But soon the road gets closer to the river and at 0.6 mile a path to the right leads down to the river's edge at a broad pool great for swimming or trout fishing. At 1.1 miles the road crosses a bridge over a side stream. Watch for another path right down to the river at 1.3 miles; here the river drops through several pools. At this path to the right, the road curves left away from the river.

At 1.4 miles, where the road curves right, is a junction. (The Upper Dark Hollow Trail leads to the left, ascending Dark Hollow to emerge on a road at 0.7 mile. To the left, the road exits from the park and passes the Potomac Appalachian Trail Club's Meadows Cabin—for members only—finally reaching VA 648. To the right, the road continues as a trail through a section of the Rapidan Wildlife Management Area to connect in 2.0 miles with the Rapidan Fire Road, hike 50.) Stay to the right on the Rose River Fire Road as it continues up the mountain.

Watch for a large white pine and, in summer, wild raspberries along the road. At 4.0 miles, a post on the left marks an unmaintained path on the right that leads down to the Rose River Loop; this is not recommended. Where the road curves right at 4.7 miles, you'll reach another junction (the Stony Mountain Trail on the left ascends the steep slope of Stony Mountain to emerge on the Rapidan Fire Road, hike 50, in 1.1 miles); continue straight ahead on the fire road.

The Rose River Fire Road then continues up to another junction (the Rose River Loop, hike 43, is to the right); continue straight ahead. The road then crosses Hogcamp Branch on a metal bridge at 5.6 miles. On the other side, the Dark Hollow Falls Trail (hike 45) leads up to the left; stay straight.

Continuing, you'll pass the Cave Cemetery on the left and reach Skyline Drive at Fishers Gap at 6.6 miles. (The Skyland–Big Meadows Horse Trail, hike 31, crosses the road just before the drive. The horse trail to the north/right is the beginning of the Rose River Loop; to the south/left, the horse trail heads toward its southern terminus at Big Meadows.)

THE BIG MEADOWS AREA

The dedication of Shenandoah National Park by President Roosevelt in 1936 took place at Big Meadows, a large open area that lies across Skyline Drive from the Henry F. Byrd Sr. Visitor Center. The visitor center is named for the Virginia governor, and later U.S. senator, who supported the establishment of the park and appointed the Virginia Conservation and Development Commission, which purchased the land for the park. Byrd Visitor Center has an outside balcony and large windows overlooking Skyline Drive and Big Meadows. At Big Meadows you'll also find a picnic area, campground, lodge, and wayside.

Perhaps first cleared by Native Americans and later enlarged by settlers for cattle grazing, Big Meadows was once much larger, the forest now having reclaimed much of the open area. The park staff maintains Big Meadows at its current 119 acres as a shrub/meadows community with a 25-acre wetland.

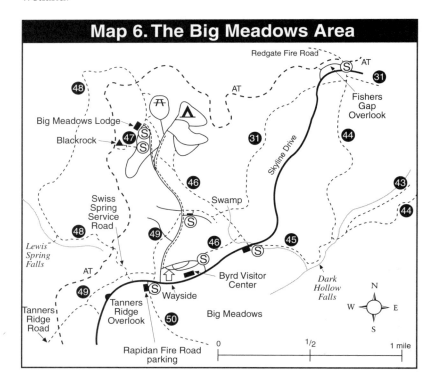

Map 6. The Big Meadows Area

Skyline Drive: Approaching Big Meadows, Skyline Drive passes parking for Dark Hollow Falls on the left at Mile 50.7; here you can access the Dark Hollow Falls Trail (hike 45) for a walk to the cascading falls. At Mile 51.0 on the right, you'll reach the North Entrance to Big Meadows; the large meadow opens on the left side of Skyline Drive. Turn right to reach the Big Meadows services complex. From parking on the left for the Harry F. Byrd Sr. Visitor Center, you can walk to the Story-of-the-Forest Nature Trail (hike 46).

At Mile 51.2 is the South Entrance to Big Meadows; this is the road to the lodge, picnic area, and campground. Near the South Entrance is the wayside, on the right. From Big Meadows Lodge, you can hike to Blackrock Summit (hike 47) and Lewis Spring Falls (hike 48). The road to the lodge passes a parking area on the right that provides access for the Tanners Ridge Horse Trail (hike 49) and the southern end of the Skyland–Big Meadows Horse Trail (hike 31).

On Skyline Drive, just beyond the South Entrance to the Big Meadows complex, on the left at Mile 51.3, the Rapidan Fire Road (hike 50) circles Big Meadows.

45 | DARK HOLLOW FALLS TRAIL

Distance: 0.8 mile one-way
Difficulty: Moderate
Elevation loss: 600 feet
Cautions: Steep descent, popular
Connections: Story-of-the-Forest Nature Trail, Rose River
Fire Road/Rose River Loop

Attractions: This most popular trail in the park takes you by Dark Hollow Falls, the most easily accessible falls from Skyline Drive. The falls is only a short walk from Skyline Drive—so you'll probably encounter many people along the trail and sitting at the 70-foot falls.

Trailhead: Begin at the Dark Hollow Falls parking area on the left side of Skyline Drive at Mile 50.7, just before the North Entrance to the Big Meadows area. At the far left of the parking area, take the paved path down beside the drive. (You'll also see a path to the left that crosses the drive; this is a paved connector to the Story-of-the-Forest Nature Trail, hike 46, and the parking area at the Byrd Visitor Center.)

Description: As you make your way down the Dark Hollow Falls Trail, it crosses a culvert over the upper part of Hogcamp Branch, which drains the Big Meadows Swamp (the swamp lies off the nature trail on the other side of the drive). After crossing Hogcamp Branch, the path becomes a

Dark Hollow Falls

well-traveled gravel path. In your descent, you'll see rails to the right that block shortcuts; please stay on the trail. You'll also pass several benches on your way down, which you may need for short rests on the steep ascent back up.

The trail follows Hogcamp Branch downstream. The path swings right and then at 0.5 mile curves left at the confluence of a tributary of Hogcamp Branch that drains Big Meadow. You'll then follow the combined waters of Hogcamp Branch as the stream continues descending in small cascades.

At 0.6 mile the trail reaches an overlook at the top of Dark Hollow Falls on Hogcamp Branch. Continue steeply down and curve right to reach the bottom for a better look at the cascade, where water skips down the rock face.

From the base of the falls, the trail turns left to continue a steep descent along Hogcamp Branch with several cascades and small falls of water. Make a final descent with switchbacks to emerge on the Rose River Fire Road (hike 44),

Cascade seen from Dark Hollow Falls Trail

which is also part of the Rose River Loop (hike 43), at 0.8 mile.

46 | STORY-OF-THE-FOREST NATURE TRAIL

Distance: 1.8-mile loop
Difficulty: Easy
Elevation change: 150 feet
Cautions: Horse crossing
Connections: Dark Hollow Falls Trail

Attractions: This easy loop hike introduces you to the Blue Ridge forest and the unique, high-elevation Big Meadows Swamp. Hogcamp Branch emerges from the swamp, which has abundant wildflowers blooming in spring. This is a self-guiding trail with interpretive signs.

Trailhead: At Mile 51.0 on Skyline Drive, turn right into the North Entrance to the Big Meadows service complex, and then turn in at the first parking on the left, for the Byrd Visitor Center. The nature trail begins to the north across the entrance road from the parking area. (You may also access the trail at its other end in the campground and by a short walk from the Big Meadows Lodge; those access points are mentioned in the hike description that follows.)

Description: The nature trail lies at the edge of the woods on the North Entrance road. When you begin the trail, stay to the right on the paved path; straight ahead is access to a maintenance area.

Cross a stone bridge over the streambed of Hogcamp Branch at 0.2 mile and soon reach a junction (to the right, a path leads to Skyline Drive across from the Dark Hollow Falls parking area at Mile 50.7); turn left to continue on the nature trail, which is not paved from this point on.

You may see evidence of recent streambed restoration to repair erosion caused by flooding. Cross back over the streambed on a metal bridge at 0.4 mile and reach an intersection with the Skyland–Big Meadows Horse Trail. (From the right it has traveled all the way from Skyland, hike 31, and to the left it leads to a parking area and a junction with the Tanners Ridge Horse Trail, hike 49.) Stay straight on the nature trail.

In 150 yards you'll see Big Meadows Swamp to the right. Please observe from the edge of the swamp, and do not enter it; foot traffic causes soil compaction and vegetation damage in this ecologically fragile area. Continuing past Big Meadows Swamp, you reach a junction at 0.8 mile (a path straight ahead leads to the campground); turn left.

You'll come out to the campground road and connect with the paved trail that parallels the road between the campground/picnic area and the Big Meadows Wayside near the visitor center. (Just to the left, another paved path leads down from the Big Meadows Lodge.) Turn left on the paved path, which is open to bicycles.

You'll reach the Big Meadows Wayside at 1.7 miles and walk through the parking area for the Byrd Visitor Center to your starting point at 1.8 miles.

47 | BLACKROCK SUMMIT

Distance: 150 yards one-way
Difficulty: Easy
Elevation gain: 100 feet
Cautions: Rock bluff
Connections: AT

Attractions: From the summit of Blackrock, at 3,721 feet the fourth-highest peak in the park, you have a great view west. This is a good sunset spot for those staying at the Big Meadows Lodge, and the walk is a nice stroll after dinner at the lodge restaurant.

Trailhead: At Mile 51.2, turn right into the South Entrance to the Big Meadows complex. You'll pass a service center and the turn to the wayside and visitor center; keep going straight. Where the road forks to the right to the campground, stay to the left to head toward the Big Meadows Lodge, operated by ARAMARK Virginia Sky-Line Company. Enter the parking area to the left of the lodge and look for signs where the trail begins near the end of the parking area.

Description: Take the paved path from the trailhead sign through the cabin area and then up the unpaved path. The ascent is somewhat rocky. Near the summit you'll pass a communication installation on the left and then reach a trail to the left (it leads down to a junction with the service road for the installation; at that junction, you can turn right to connect with the Appalachian Trail (AT) in 0.2 mile); continue straight to a rock outcrop at the summit of Blackrock.

48 | LEWIS SPRING FALLS LOOP

Distance: 3.0 miles; Lewis Spring Falls, 1.3 miles one-way
Difficulty: Moderate
Elevation change: 800 feet
Cautions: Rocky and steep in places
Connections: AT, Lewis Spring Service Road

Attractions: This loop swings by Lewis Spring Falls, an 81-foot cascading waterfall. This is one of the most picturesque waterfalls in the park, dropping into a steep gorge.

Trailhead: At Mile 51.2, turn right into the South Entrance to the Big Meadows complex. You'll pass a service center and the turn to the wayside and visitor center; keep going straight. Where the road forks to the right to the campground and picnic area, stay to the left to head toward Big Meadows Lodge. Enter the parking area to the left of the lodge; walk to the north and look for a paved path leading into the woods at the sign that says "Big Meadows Lodge." The paved walkway to the right leads back along the road to the Big Meadows Wayside and Skyline Drive.

Description: In a short distance down the trail, you'll reach a junction (the trail straight ahead leads to the picnic area, from where you may also begin this hike; the trail to the right leads out to the campground road); turn left to head for Lewis Spring Falls. As you walk down the trail, you'll see the amphitheater on the right, from where you may also begin this hike; the amphitheater is accessed from the picnic area.

The trail intersects the Appalachian Trail at 0.1 mile (you'll complete this loop along the AT from the left; to the right, the AT leads to the Big Meadows Campground in 0.5 mile and Fishers Gap in 1.6 miles); follow the blue-blazed Lewis Spring Falls Trail straight ahead.

From the intersection with the AT, the trail descends, at times steeply, with flat rocks that you must walk across. At 0.6 mile the trail reaches a rock bluff on the left. Traverse a more open area at 1.1 miles that affords views into the valley. Step up rocks several times and then pass over a rise at 1.2 miles. Watch for a boulder sitting atop another boulder on the right.

At 1.3 miles, a 250-foot side trail to the right leads to Lewis Spring Falls. Turn on the side path and you'll soon reach an overlook that gives a grand view of the valley. From this overlook, another side trail to the right leads down to the foot of the waterfall, but the way is very steep and rocky and not recommended. Stay to the left, and the trail soon crosses the stream above the waterfall over rocks cemented together. Keep going up to a railing that takes you around to an observation point above Lewis Spring Falls.

Return to the main trail, ascending from the waterfall side path. The trail is rocky along this section. You'll soon cross the stream of Lewis Spring where it runs under the trail in a culvert. Then follow a rock bluff on the left.

The trail meanders through a series of curves and switchbacks as it ascends toward the ridgeline. At 1.7 miles, where an abandoned section of trail leads straight, turn right. You'll pass a side path to the right that leads to an open, level area. At 1.9 miles the trail reaches a junction (an old road leads to the left); turn right on the old roadbed to continue.

Here the way is graveled. You'll pass the pumping station for the Big Meadows area water supply on the left, a bermed structure with a locked door. Then pass a side path that leads to Lewis Spring, the source of the stream that forms Lewis Spring Falls. At 2.0 miles, ascend to a crossing of the AT. (Straight ahead, you can walk the Lewis Spring Service Road 0.2 mile out to Skyline Drive at Mile 51.4; to the right, the AT crosses Tanners Ridge Road in 0.6 mile and then crosses Skyline Drive at Milam Gap in 1.7 miles.) Turn left on the AT to complete this loop hike.

Along the AT, you'll pass under powerlines leading down to the pumping station you passed earlier. The trail ascends, rocky in places; cross an old roadbed, now faint. At 2.4 miles there is a side path to the right (it leads 0.2 mile up to the summit of Blackrock; from there it is a short walk down the other side to the parking lot for the lodge); continue straight to complete this loop.

The AT passes below Blackrock and then behind the lodge, which you can see through the trees. You'll reach the junction with the Lewis Spring Falls Trail at 2.9 miles to close the loop; turn right to get back to the trailhead and Big Meadows Lodge.

49 | TANNERS RIDGE HORSE TRAIL

Distance: 1.1 miles one-way
Difficulty: Easy
Elevation change: 100 feet
Cautions: Can get overgrown
Connections: Skyland–Big Meadows Horse Trail, Rapidan
Fire Road, Tanners Ridge Road, AT

Attractions: This horse trail provides a short connector from the Big Meadows area to the Rapidan and Tanners Ridge Roads.

Trailhead: At Mile 51.2, turn right into the South Entrance of the Big Meadows complex and head straight, toward the lodge. Pass the service center and the turn to the wayside and visitor center on the right; keep going straight. You'll then pass on the left a road into a wastewater treatment plant; at the next road, turn right, toward the ranger maintenance area, and pull into the parking area on the left.

Description: At the far east end of the parking area, follow a service road into the woods. Soon you'll encounter a horse trail crossing the service road. This is actually a junction of trails. (To the right the Skyland–Big Meadows Horse Trail (hike 31) leads 11.3 miles north to Skyland; this is the southern terminus of that horse trail.) Turn left here on the Tanners Ridge Horse Trail.

At 0.1 mile you'll cross the main road leading to the lodge, and bear left into the woods away from a side road leading into a residence area. The trail crosses the paved road that leads to the wastewater treatment plant at 0.4 mile. Descend into the woods, where you'll see to the right an overgrown roadway that leads to the treatment plant. Just beyond is the junction of a return loop of the trail; it's not easy to spot, so you may pass right by it. This return portion of the loop is no longer maintained and has become too overgrown to follow.

This stretch of woods is a favorite deer haunt, so you'll see several standing in the woods or on the trail watching you. At 0.6 mile, there's a path to the left (it leads up to hitching rails and picnic tables; horse riders can leave horses here to walk up to the wayside and visitor center); continue straight.

You'll reach boulders in the trail; if you pass straight ahead through these boulders, you emerge on Skyline Drive across from the Rapidan Fire Road (hike 50); to continue the Tanners Ridge Horse Trail, turn to the right just before the boulders.

At 0.8 mile, there's a junction where the old loop comes together at its middle; stay to the left and you'll soon cross the Lewis Spring Service Road (to the left it leads to Skyline Drive and to the right to Lewis Spring Falls, hike 48); go straight ahead.

Back into the woods, the trail passes through an overgrown area and emerges on Tanners Ridge Road at 1.1 miles. (To the right the road heads down the mountain to emerge from the park and connect with VA 682 in 1.2 miles; just down the Tanners Ridge Road, the Appalachian Trail crosses near the large Thomas/Meadows Cemetery, still used. To the left, Tanners Ridge Road leads up to Skyline Drive in 0.2 mile at Mile 51.6. Although this road is gated at both ends, you may encounter vehicles along here because the road is used by park employees who live in the valley.)

50 | RAPIDAN FIRE ROAD

Distance: 10.5 miles one-way; Rapidan Camp, 1.0-mile side trip
Difficulty: Moderate
Elevation loss: 2,500 feet
Cautions: Rocky
Connections: Mill Prong Horse Trail, Stony Mountain Trail, Upper Dark Hollow Trail, Rapidan Camp

Attractions: This road offers a brief mountain bike ride and access to Rapidan Camp, a fishing retreat established in 1929 by former President Herbert Hoover in a hemlock glade at the confluence of Laurel Prong and Mill Prong. These streams form the Rapidan River; originally pronounced "Rapid Anne," the river was named by colonial governor Alexander Spotswood for Britain's Queen Anne. President Hoover donated "Camp Rapidan," as he called it, to the national park at the end of his term in office. Consisting of thirteen structures, it was known as "Camp Hoover" for a time, until it recently was given back the original name, although changed to "Rapidan Camp" so as not to confuse it with a Camp Rapidan outside the park. Only three structures remain, including the president's cabin, which was called "Brown House." The camp is still available to government officials to use as a retreat.

Trailhead: At Mile 51.3, just past the Big Meadows South Entrance, turn left onto the Rapidan Fire Road. There's ample parking. The road is gated just beyond the parking; on Rapidan Camp Day in the summer, bus tours from the Byrd Visitor Center drive down to the camp. Beyond the parking, the road is open to hikers, horses, and, for the first mile, bicycles; this is the only trail section in the park open to bikes, other than the paved trail from the Big Meadows lodge/campground to the Byrd Visitor Center. When

Rapidan Fire Road emerges from the park, it becomes VA 649, which can be reached off VA 670 west of Criglersville.

Description: Proceed up the Rapidan Fire Road. The road circles the south end of Big Meadows before entering the woods at 0.6 mile. This is a popular walk for viewing the meadows and the abundant wildlife you'll see there at the end of the day—numerous deer and an occasional black bear.

A side road to the left at 1.0 mile leads to a stone dumping area. At another road to the left at 1.1 miles, bikes must turn around because they are not allowed farther down the road. At 1.2 miles, the Mill Prong Horse Trail turns off to the right, leading down toward Rapidan Camp; this trail is very rocky and eroded. Continue straight on Rapidan Fire Road.

Begin a descent of the mountain. At 3.0 miles, the Stony Mountain Trail lies to the left (it leads 1.1 miles to connect with the Rose River Fire Road, hike 44); stay straight.

At 4.0 miles, the Upper Dark Hollow Trail begins on the left (it also connects with the Rose River Fire Road, in 2.0 miles); stay straight on the Rapidan Fire Road here too.

At 5.9 miles, you reach a junction. A road to the right leads 0.5 mile to Rapidan Camp. After the short side trip to the camp, return to the Rapidan Fire Road, and now go straight to continue the hike.

This section of the Rapidan Fire Road was once the Criglersville Road and would have been the route used by President Hoover to enter the area. At 6.3 miles, the road is gated where it enters a section of the Rapidan Wildlife Management Area (WMA). Before emerging from the wildlife management area, the road crosses the Rapidan on a bridge. At 8.0 miles, near the east boundary of the WMA, there is a junction (the Fork Mountain Road to the left leads southwest to a radio tower); the Rapidan Fire Road continues straight along the river through another section of the park.

At 9.3 miles, you'll reach a fork. (The Lower Rapidan Fire Road to the right leads southeast 1.7 miles to emerge from the park as VA 662 and head toward Graves Mill; this lower portion of the fire road was destroyed by flooding the summer of 1995 and will eventually be reconstructed as a horse trail and called the "Rapidan Trail.") Go to the left on the fork that climbs from the river to a junction on Chapman Mountain (the Blakey Ridge Fire Road leads to the right to a lookout tower outside the park). Continue straight on the Chapman Mountain Road to emerge from the park at 10.5 miles, where Chapman Mountain Road becomes VA 649, the Rapidan–Criglersville Road.

BIG MEADOWS TO LEWIS MOUNTAIN

Between Big Meadows and Lewis Mountain, Skyline Drive passes through a couple of gaps. Milam Gap is probably where colonial governor Alexander Spotswood and his "Knights of the Horseshoe" crossed the Blue Ridge in their exploration of the mountains in the early 1700s. Bootens Gap is where the Fairfax Line, marking the southwest boundary of the lands of Lord Fairfax, crossed the mountain ridge. Hikes in this section lead to President Hoover's Rapidan Camp, several mountain peaks, and the streams of Laurel Prong and Devils Ditch. At Lewis Mountain, you'll find camping, picnicking, cabins, and a camp store.

Skyline Drive: Continue south from Big Meadows, passing the Rapidan Fire Road on the left. Skyline Drive reaches the Lewis Spring Service Road on the right at Mile 51.4; the road leads 0.2 mile down to connect with the Lewis Spring Falls Trail for the shortest access to Lewis Spring Falls, 0.9 mile. There's parking beside the service road.

The Tanners Ridge Overlook at Mile 51.5 on the right offers a view west, with Tanners Ridge in the foreground, descending from the left, and the town of Stanley to the far right. At Mile 51.6 the Tanners Ridge Road on the right heads down the mountain for access to the Tanners Ridge Horse Trail (hike 49); where the Appalachian Trail (AT) crosses the road, 0.3 mile down from Skyline Drive, lies the Thomas/Meadows Cemetery, still maintained and used. The drive passes through Milam Gap at Mile 52.8, where you can pick up the AT, which crosses the drive in the gap and connects with the Mill Prong Trail (hike 51) for a walk to Rapidan Camp.

The Naked Creek Overlook on the right at Mile 53.2 offers a view down the hollow of Naked Creek. The Hazeltop Ridge Overlook lies on the right side of Skyline Drive at Mile 54.4; the long ridge running across the foreground of the view is, in fact, Long Ridge. The Powell Mountain Trail (hike 52) leads from the overlook to Powell Mountain, which stands to the left. Skyline Drive passes through Bootens Gap at Mile 55.1, where the Conway River Fire Road heads east and you can pick up the AT for access to the Laurel Prong Trail (hike 53).

At Mile 55.6 at The Point Overlook, look to the far right to see Hazeltop. You can take a path straight out from the overlook 100 yards to a rock outcrop offering a view west that is one of the best in the park, with ridge after ridge stretching into the distance.

Parking on the right at Mile 56.4 offers access to Bearfence Mountain (hike 54). Continuing south from Bearfence Mountain parking, you'll reach the Slaughter Fire Road (hike 55) to the east at Mile 56.8.

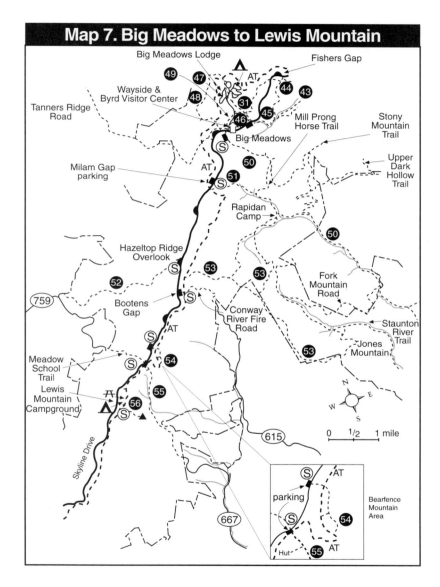

Map 7. Big Meadows to Lewis Mountain

At Mile 57.5, the Lewis Mountain Campground complex lies to the left. As you turn into the campground entrance, stay to the right to pass the picnic area on the left, and then pass cabins and the camp store, operated by the concessionaire. Beyond the store is the campground, where you can select a site and then sign up at the self-registration station. At the back of the campground you can access the Lewis Mountain Trail (hike 56).

51 | MILL PRONG TRAIL TO RAPIDAN CAMP

Distance: 1.8 miles one-way; Big Rock Falls, 1.5 miles one-way; President's Walk/Fisherman's Loop, 1.0-mile side trip
Difficulty: Moderate
Elevation loss: 800 feet
Cautions: Creek fords
Connections: AT, Mill Prong Horse Trail, Laurel Prong Trail

Attractions: This trail descends along Mill Prong past Big Rock Falls for the shortest access to Rapidan Camp. You are free to explore the compound, which includes three of the original cabins, including the President's Cabin, but stay at a distance if the cabins are occupied. An outdoor fireplace and a stone fountain still stand on the grounds. The other structures were dismantled because of a lack of funds to renovate and maintain them. The remaining buildings and the landscaping recently have been renovated and restored to their original appearance. During the years President Hoover used the camp, a marine camp housed troops to the east and a cabinet members camp was located farther down the Rapidan. The president's camp sits above the confluence of Mill Prong with Laurel Prong; the two create the Rapidan River.

This is a good walk for wildflowers in the spring. A profusion of wildflowers covers the ground, some planted during the time the Hoovers occupied the camp. Landscaping the area kept Mrs. Hoover busy while the president was fly-fishing. Lou Henry Hoover and her gardeners worked to increase the number of herbaceous wildflowers in the area. Today, there are nearly twice the number of wildflowers, especially wood aster, sweet cicely, and showy orchis.

Trailhead: In Milam Gap, at Mile 52.8, turn into the parking area on the right. Notice the apple trees here; the apples of Joseph Milam were well known for keeping well through the winter and making fine brandy.

Description: To the left of the parking area, access the Appalachian Trail and turn left, to cross Skyline Drive and at 0.1 mile reach a junction (straight ahead on the AT, the summit of Hazeltop Mountain is in 1.9 miles, at 3,812 feet the third-highest peak in the park; since the top is forested, there is no view); turn left on the Mill Prong Trail.

President's Cabin at Camp Hoover

Pass through the old Milam apple orchard on a wide path. At 0.4 mile begin a descent into the hollow of Mill Prong. The trail turns left at 0.6 mile, where the path straight ahead has been abandoned. Soon after, descend to a ford of Mill Prong. Walk up from the creek and then descend again to rockhop a side stream at 1.0 mile and reach a junction (the Mill Prong Horse Trail leads left 1.0 mile up to the Rapidan Fire Road, hike 50, and provides horse access from Big Meadows); bear right, with the hiking and horse trails now coinciding.

The trail bears left to once more parallel the cascading Mill Prong. Begin a steeper descent at 1.4 miles, with switchbacks right and left, and descend to Big Rock Falls on Mill Prong at 1.5 miles, a short cascade. Ford the creek below the falls and turn to the right uphill, instead of staying straight along the creek.

Soon the trail descends along the creek again through a hemlock forest to emerge on the Rapidan Camp Road at 1.8 miles. The summer camp of President Herbert Hoover lies across the road. To get oriented, turn right on the camp road for 100 yards to a path to the left, which takes you

Map of Camp Hoover

by a display board showing a map of the compound. To the right, the Laurel Prong Trail (hike 53) heads south. Ahead, you'll see the President's Cabin (originally called "Brown House") and to the right the Prime Minister's Cabin, named for Britain's Prime Minister, Ramsay McDonald, who came to Rapidan Camp to confer with the U.S. president on limiting the building of naval warships. To the far left of the compound sits the Creel Cabin.

From beside the Prime Minister's Cabin, the 1.0-mile President's Walk/Fisherman's Loop leads up to Hemlock Run, a man-made run that once diverted water from Laurel Prong. The trail continues up the run to Laurel Prong, where the small Laurel Dam controlled the water in Hemlock Run. The Fisherman's Loop continues up Laurel Prong. The trail eventually curves right and ascends to a junction with the Laurel Prong Trail; turn right to complete the loop back to Rapidan Camp.

52 | POWELL MOUNTAIN TRAIL

**Distance: 3.6 miles one-way; summit of Powell
  Mountain, 2.0 miles one-way**
Difficulty: Moderate
Elevation loss: 2,000 feet; elevation change to Powell
  Mountain summit, 500 feet
Cautions: Can get overgrown, some erosion
Connections: None

Attractions: A cool, pleasant walk through wildflowers in late summer, with stands of boneset blossoming white, leads over the summit of Powell Mountain. In summer you'll see many spotted star-thistle with purple-pink flowers, a nonnative plant that grows in open areas.

Trailhead: At Mile 54.4, turn into the Hazeltop Ridge Overlook on the right side of Skyline Drive. A gap in the rock wall at the overlook is the beginning of the Powell Mountain Trail.

Description: Walk through the gap and bear left across the open area below the overlook. At 0.1 mile the trail enters the woods. Bear right in a moderately steep descent that winds through the forest. At 0.6 mile, watch for the trail to jog to the right as you drop into a saddle between the main Blue Ridge and Powell Mountain. The trail heads up the flank of Powell Mountain to reach the ridgeline and bears left to top the first peak at 0.9 mile. The trail then descends the steep, rocky west slope. Keep an eye on the blazes to stay on the path.

The trail curves to the right through a wash and drops into another sag at 1.8 miles among tall poplars. You'll ascend over the summit of Powell Mountain at 2.0 miles; because the top is forested, there are no views. The trail then begins a long winding descent of the southwest slope, emerging from the park and connecting with VA 759 at 3.6 miles.

53 LAUREL PRONG, FORK MOUNTAIN, JONES MOUNTAIN, AND CAT KNOB TRAILS

Distance: 7.1-mile loop
Difficulty: Moderate
Elevation change: 1,000 feet
Cautions: Steep ascent and descent, creek ford, trail erosion
Connections: AT, Rapidan Camp, Fork Mountain Road

Attractions: This loop provides an isolated hike through the park's remote backcountry. The route descends along Laurel Prong, lined with mountain laurel, and ascends to "The Sag," a gap between Fork Mountain and Jones Mountain that separates the Staunton River watershed from the Laurel Prong watershed.

Trailhead: Turn into the parking area on the left side of Skyline Drive at Bootens Gap at Mile 55.1.

Description: Begin on the Conway River Fire Road, which heads east, straight into the woods. In a few paces, you'll reach an intersection with the Appalachian Trail. (To the right, the AT leads 11.6 miles south to Swift Run Gap. Straight ahead, the fire road continues southeast to leave the park in 1.4 miles and pass through a section of the Rapidan Wildlife Management Area, becoming VA 615, which leads toward the Graves Mill community—Francis Conway settled the area in the early 1700s.) Turn left to head north on the AT.

Ascend to a junction at 0.5 mile (straight ahead, the AT continues north, in 0.5 mile crossing over Hazeltop Mountain and reaching Milam Gap in another 1.9 miles); turn right on the Laurel Prong Trail.

The trail moves down and up along the slope of the mountain to descend at 1.4 miles to a level area. It then descends to Laurel Gap at 1.5 miles. Here you'll encounter the loop, with the Cat Knob Trail, which is your return route, straight ahead; turn left to stay on the Laurel Prong Trail.

The trail descends through an area called "The Laurels" for the profusion of mountain laurel. At 1.7 miles you'll pass a cut log on the left that makes a nice bench for a rest stop. The trail then descends through a hemlock woods; grouse burst from cover along this beautiful trail. Watch for a large hemlock to the right at 2.0 miles. You'll pass through a bottomland of ferns and then a large hemlock on the left.

The trail crosses several shallow side streams that feed the Laurel Prong to your right. Through this lowland watch for stacks of rocks left from when the area was settled. At 2.4 miles, step over a stream flowing from a spring to the left of the trail.

At 2.8 miles, you'll reach a junction (the Laurel Prong Trail continues straight here as a horse trail to reach Rapidan Camp in another 0.6 mile); turn right on the Fork Mountain Trail to continue the loop.

You'll recross the small stream from above and then ford Laurel Prong at 2.9 miles. Following an old roadbed, the trail then makes a steep and nearly continuous ascent up Fork Mountain to reach a junction at 4.1 miles in "The Sag." (Straight ahead you can walk out to the Fork Mountain Road. To the left, Fork Mountain Road leads up to an FAA radio tower; the summit also served as a signal point for both armies in the Civil War. President Hoover had a lookout tower at the summit while he occupied his camp on the Rapidan. To the right, Fork Mountain Road leads east, passing the Staunton River Trail along the way, which heads east to pass Jones Mountain and connect with the Lower Rapidan Fire Road, which becomes VA 662 when it emerges from the park; the Fork Mountain Road then heads north to enter the Rapidan Wildlife Management Area and connect with the Rapidan Fire Road, hike 50. On Jones Mountain stands the Jones Mountain Cabin, originally built by Albert Nichols in 1855 and restored by the Potomac Appalachian Trail Club; the mountain bears the name of David Jones, who lived in the area in the 1740s. The Staunton River Valley includes 1,000 acres of old-growth forest; only dead standing chestnut was taken in 1938 to build the cabins and lodge at Big Meadows. The flood of 1995 damaged the Staunton River Trail, washing away most of it from Jones Mountain east, but the trail has since been rerouted and repaired.) From the junction in The Sag, turn right on the Jones Mountain Trail to head south.

This trail can get a bit overgrown in summer. In fall watch for large stands of blue cohosh with its blue berries; tall ferns are scattered among mountain laurel. The trail mostly ascends, finally climbing steeply to a junction near the top of Cat Knob at 5.1 miles (the Jones Mountain Trail continues to the left, heading east to pass Bear Church Rock on Jones Mountain and connect with the Staunton River Trail); turn right on the Cat Knob Trail.

Ascend over Cat Knob, make a steep descent to Laurel Gap at 5.6 miles, and reach the junction with the Laurel Prong Trail to close the loop. Continue straight on the Laurel Prong Trail to ascend to the AT, where you turn left to get back to Bootens Gap at 7.1 miles.

54 | BEARFENCE MOUNTAIN LOOP

**Distance: 1.2 miles; Bearfence Mountain Summit,
0.3 mile one-way**
Difficulty: Strenuous
Elevation change: 300 feet
Cautions: Steep drop-offs, rock scramble
Connections: AT

Attractions: This short hike offers a grand view from the top of Bearfence Mountain. The Bearfence Rocks along the summit ridge appear to form a fence along the top of the mountain, hence the name. At several places along this trail and many other places in the park in summer, you'll find large patches of spotted jewelweed blooming orange. These flowers belong to the touch-me-not family, so named because in late summer when you touch the mature seed pods, they pop open, throwing out their seeds.

Trailhead: At Mile 56.4 along Skyline Drive, you'll find parking for Bearfence Mountain on the right side of the road. To get to the trail, you must cross the drive to the east side, where you'll see a sign indicating the Bearfence Rocks in 300 yards.

Description: The trail ascends from Skyline Drive into a hardwood forest with ferns carpeting the forest floor. In 100 yards, the trail crosses the Appalachian Trail (to the right it is the return part of this loop; to the left, the AT leads north 1.4 miles to Bootens Gap and the Conway River Fire Road); continue straight on the Bearfence Mountain Loop.

The trail passes a large rock and at 0.1 mile begins ascending through rocks as it circles to the south. At 300 yards you'll reach two outcroppings that are the first of the Bearfence Rocks along the ridge of Bearfence Mountain. The trail descends and turns to the right to pass over another outcrop. You'll see on the left a place where people have tried to bushwhack around, but the trail actually goes directly up over the rocks.

The trail drops to the ground again and passes more outcroppings, until at 0.3 mile you'll climb to the summit of Bearfence Mountain. Halfway up, there's a double blaze indicating a turn up through the rocks to the top. Steep drop-offs plunge down to your right; be careful and do not attempt this climb when the rocks are wet and slippery.

The summit offers a 360-degree view of the surrounding mountains and valleys. To the southwest, you'll see a portion of Skyline Drive and to the west across the Shenandoah Valley, Massanutten Mountain. To the east, you'll see the Conway River Valley with Jones and Bluff Mountains beyond.

The trail from the summit continues south along the ridgeline. Descend and drop off to the right to continue along the trail. At 0.4 mile is a junction (a short connector to the right leads less than 100 yards to the AT; you can return along this connector if you want to shorten your loop by 0.3 mile); to walk the longer loop, continue straight past this junction.

Ascend to a viewpoint to the west. The trail then cuts across the ridgeline and descends to a junction with the AT at 0.5 mile (to the left, the AT leads 0.6 mile to the Slaughter Fire Road, hike 55); turn right on the AT to complete the loop.

You'll now be following white blazes. The trail descends gradually until at 0.7 mile you'll reach a junction with the other end of the short connector you passed earlier; continue straight on the AT. At 1.1 miles you'll return to the junction near the beginning of the hike, where the Bearfence Mountain Loop crossed the AT; turn left to cross Skyline Drive and return to the parking area.

55 | SLAUGHTER FIRE ROAD

Distance: 3.8 miles one-way
Difficulty: Moderate
Elevation loss: 1,700 feet
Cautions: Can be overgrown, creek crossing
Connections: AT, Meadow School Trail

Attractions: You'll enjoy an isolated walk down an old fire road along Devils Ditch, a tributary of the Conway River. The grassy roadbed can get overgrown, but if it has been mowed recently, the road offers a pleasant stroll through isolated backcountry. In June you'll see plenty of blooming mountain laurel. Oaks stand along the fire road, and in years when there is a good mast crop, acorns crunch and pop underfoot and even bounce off your head.

Trailhead: At Mile 56.8 on Skyline Drive, turn left onto the Slaughter Fire Road. Pass a crossing of the Appalachian Trail and find parking 100 yards from the drive. (North on the AT, it's 7.8 miles to Big Meadows, and to the south it's 9.3 miles to Swift Run Gap. To access the Meadow School Trail, which follows an old road down the mountain on the west to emerge from the park in 1.4 miles as VA 759, you would walk back up the fire road and cross Skyline Drive.)

Description: Head down the Slaughter Fire Road. At 0.2 mile, the road passes another roadway to the right, which leads 0.1 mile to the Bearfence Mountain Hut, where you can camp (reservations required). Continue straight on the Slaughter Road amid tall oaks.

A tall hemlock on the right at 0.7 mile sits on the edge of Devils Ditch. The road descends to a crossing of the stream at 0.9 mile. Recent floods have washed away a culvert and the road, so you must rockhop the stream to regain the road on the other side.

The road follows Devils Ditch downstream as it grows ever deeper. You'll eventually skirt a segment of the Rapidan Wildlife Management Area and emerge from the park to connect with VA 667 at the Conway River at 3.8 miles; access there is limited and not recommended.

56 | LEWIS MOUNTAIN TRAIL

Distance: 0.5 mile one-way
Difficulty: Easy, then strenuous
Elevation gain: 160 feet
Cautions: Overgrown beyond the summit
Connections: AT

Attractions: Lewis Mountain is named for John Lewis, a surveyor with George Washington who had a grant of land on the mountain. If you're camping at the Lewis Mountain Campground, this trail makes a pleasant walk before you settle in for the night.

Trailhead: At Mile 57.5, turn left into the Lewis Mountain complex; continue straight, past the picnic area, cabins, and camp store, to the campground. In the campground, walk to the far left corner to campsite 16; you'll see a concrete post marking the beginning of the Lewis Mountain Trail. (If you are not staying at the Lewis Mountain Campground, you can also reach the trail by entering the picnic area and, at about three-fourths of the way around the one-way loop road, access the Appalachian Trail by a 120-yard path to the right; then turn south on the AT to its junction with the Lewis Mountain Trail, described below.)

Description: Head straight into the woods from the edge of the campground. In 50 yards, you'll cross the AT (to the left, the AT passes near the Lewis Mountain picnic area; to the right, the AT continues south to Swift Run Gap); continue straight on the Lewis Mountain Trail.

Just past the junction with the AT, you'll pass an elevation marker in the middle of the trail. At a path to the right at 0.2 mile, stay left. The Lewis Mountain Trail ascends a rocky slope and then makes a more gradual ascent to the level, forested top of Lewis Mountain at 0.5 mile. (The trail continues to descend the eastern flank of Lewis Mountain, but soon gets overgrown and eventually disappears.)

LEWIS MOUNTAIN TO SWIFT RUN GAP

This southernmost section of the Central District offers hikes to the site of the Pocosin Mission and two waterfalls, Dry Run and South River, as well as Saddleback Mountain. Camping and picnicking are available at Lewis Mountain Campground.

The Central District ends at Swift Run Gap, where US 33 crosses the mountain range. The highway is also called the "Spotswood Trail" because it was thought to be the gap where colonial governor Alexander Spotswood crossed the Blue Ridge on his notorious expedition to explore the western part of the Virginia colony. The Spotswood group may have actually crossed the Blue Ridge farther to the north at Milam Gap. In Swift Run Gap along US 33, you'll see three monuments to the Spotswood expedition.

The road through Swift Run Gap was an early passage over the Blue Ridge. Improved and made a turnpike in the early 1800s, the road was used by Shenandoah Valley farmers to haul their products east, and it was also traversed by armies during the Civil War. Lam's Mill stood on the lower east side of the gap along the highway in the early 1900s; it became a gathering place for farmers needing to grind corn and wheat. Once the automobile came along, the Haney store (which stood in the gap at about where the park entrance station is today) added gas pumps, and the Murphy gas station was erected on the other side of the highway. On the lower west side of the gap, the brick Mountain Inn, later known as the Shipp Tavern, operated in the 1800s.

Skyline Drive: From Lewis Mountain south along Skyline Drive, notice how the trees branch across the road, forming a canopy. From the Oaks Overlook on the right at Mile 59.1, you can see the town of Elkton to the left. The Pocosin Fire Road on the left at Mile 59.5 leads east from the drive, providing access to the Pocosin Trail (hike 57) and the site of the Pocosin Mission. From the Baldface Mountain Overlook on the right at Mile 61.3, you can see Elkton to the left and Dean Mountain, the low ridge in the foreground. Then at Mile 62.7, you'll pass the Dry Run Falls Fire Road (hike 58) on the right and reach the South River Overlook on the left. The view from the overlook includes South River Valley to the left and Saddleback Mountain to the right. Just beyond the South River Overlook, the entrance to the South River Picnic Area lies on the left side of the drive at Mile 62.8; in the picnic area lies the trailhead for the South River Falls Loop (hike 59) and a hike to Saddleback Mountain (hike 60).

At Mile 63.1 you'll pass the service road on the left that leads to the Appalachian Trail (AT) near the beginning of the Saddleback Mountain

Trail (hike 60). Parking for the Dean cemetery lies on the right side of the drive at Mile 63.2.

The Hensley Hollow Overlook on the right at Mile 64.4 offers a view down Hensley Hollow. A pullout lies on the right at Mile 64.9. At mile 65.5, the drive enters Swift Run Gap and connects with US 33.

To the west on US 33, you can descend into Elkton for services and accommodations. On the east side of the park, you'll find a few additional services in Stanardsville. Passing through Swift Run Gap, Skyline Drive continues into the South District of the national park.

57   POCOSIN FIRE ROAD AND POCOSIN TRAIL

Distance: 2.7 miles one-way; Pocosin Mission Ruins, 1.1 miles one-way; South River cemetery, 0.2-mile side trip
Difficulty: Moderate
Elevation loss: 800 feet
Cautions: Can be overgrown, severe flood damage
Connections: AT, Pocosin Hollow Trail, South River Fire Road

Attractions: This route leads by the ruins of an Episcopal mission and the South River cemetery. The mission was established in 1904 to work within the mountain community that once occupied this area of the park. Pocosin is an Indian word meaning "swamp" or "marsh." The trail reaches the South River Fire Road, which can be used for a loop hike.

Trailhead: At Mile 59.5, turn left onto the Pocosin Fire Road, where you'll find parking.

Description: Walk down the Pocosin Fire Road. At 0.1 mile, the road crosses the AT (to the left, you can walk 1.7 miles to a junction with the Lewis Mountain Trail, hike 56, at the Lewis Mountain Campground; to the right, the AT leads 2.9 miles to the South River Fire Road); keep straight past the AT.

At 0.2 mile, a side road to the right leads up to the Pocosin Cabin, built by the Civilian Conservation Corps and now maintained by the Potomac Appalachian Trail Club (the cabin may be rented); continue straight on the Pocosin Fire Road.

Descend to a junction at 1.1 miles. (The fire road continues straight. In 0.2 mile on the left, the Pocosin Hollow Trail heads north and east to descend Pocosin Hollow, crossing the stream and emerging from the park in 2.1 miles, crossing the stream again, and connecting with VA 667 at 2.8 miles; most of this trail was washed out in a 1995 flood, so take care if you explore this region. The Pocosin Fire Road itself continues east to reach the

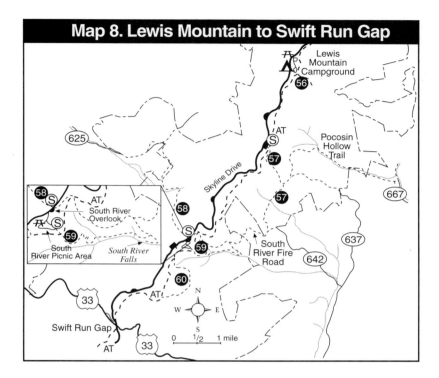

Map 8. Lewis Mountain to Swift Run Gap

park boundary in 1.2 miles and head southeast as VA 637.) At the junction, turn right onto the Pocosin Trail.

Immediately to the left, you'll see the tumble-down ruins of a wooden cabin. Beyond lie the foundations of the old stone Pocosin Mission, with steps leading up to the nonexistent door. Across the trail from the mission site, you'll find the few nameless headstones of an old cemetery.

Continue down the Pocosin Trail, following an old roadbed. The trail can get quite overgrown in late summer. You'll step over several small streams. At 2.1 miles, the trail passes over a rise, drops into a hollow, and curves left at a large poplar tree, where a stream emerges from rocks below the trail. Here you'll see some of the largest trees in the park.

At 2.6 miles, a side trail to the left leads 0.1 mile to the South River cemetery. This side trail can also be overgrown in summer. Watch for a curve left before you reach the fenced cemetery. You'll find grave markers from the 1800s.

Back on the main trail, turn right after the cemetery to complete the hike. At 2.7 miles, the trail ends at the South River Fire Road at the park boundary. (To the left, the South River Fire Road becomes VA 642, which at this writing

Pocosin Mission ruins

is closed for public access. To the right, the South River Fire Road leads past the South River Falls Loop, hike 59, and intersects the AT near Skyline Drive at the South River Overlook at Mile 62.7.)

You can use the South River Fire Road to complete a 7.7-mile loop hike. Turn right on the South River Road, walk along the park boundary and pass through part of the Rapidan Wildlife Management Area before reentering the park. This road also can get overgrown in late summer. Continuing on the road, you reach another road to the left at 3.9 miles; to the left, you can reach the end of the South River Falls Trail in 0.4 mile—it's then 0.2 mile up that trail to the overlook for South River Falls, hike 59; to complete this suggested loop hike, stay to the right and continue up the South River Fire Road. At 4.7 miles you reach a junction with the AT; left on the AT leads 0.5 mile to the beginning of the South River Falls Trail; straight on the road leads to Skyline Drive in 0.3 mile and Dry Run Falls Fire Road, hike 58, on the other side; turn right on the AT to complete the loop to the Pocosin Fire Road at 7.6 miles. Turn left up the road, and it's 0.1 mile back to the parking area.

58 | DRY RUN FALLS FIRE ROAD

Distance: 1.9 miles one-way; Dry Run Falls, 1.2-mile side trip
Difficulty: Easy on the road, strenuous to the falls
Elevation loss: 600 feet
Cautions: Off-trail bushwhacking necessary to see falls
Connections: AT, South River Fire Road

Attractions: Dry Run Falls is worth the trouble if you're an experienced hiker; all others may enjoy an easy stroll down the road, but do not attempt this search for the falls.

Trailhead: At Mile 62.7, pull into the South River Overlook on the left, where you can park.

Description: From the South River Overlook parking, walk back up Skyline Drive to the South River Fire Road, which leads 0.3 mile to the Appalachian Trail (AT) and the South River Falls Loop (hike 59); cross the drive to head down the Dry Run Falls Fire Road.

At 0.7 mile watch for rock outcrops on the right and a tall cliff. At 1.3 miles the road crosses Dry Run and then bears left to follow the creek downstream. At 1.9 miles, you'll reach a chain across the road blocking vehicle access from outside the park (the road continues, emerging from the park to connect with VA 625 in another mile, but the road condition is poor and there's no parking on this lower end); just before the chain across the road, turn left to follow an old roadbed.

Stay with it, and you'll reach the edge of Dry Run at 2.3 miles. You must then bushwhack your way down Dry Run until you reach the falls at 2.5 miles. You'll pass some spillways in the creek as you descend, but keep going until you reach a cascade of about 20 feet. Because of the off-trail search for the falls, this route should only be attempted by experienced hikers.

59 | SOUTH RIVER FALLS LOOP

Distance: 4.7 miles; South River Falls Overlook, 1.3 miles one-way
Difficulty: Moderate
Elevation change: 1,000 feet
Cautions: Steep downhill
Connections: AT, South River Fire Road

Attractions: This hike descends to an overlook of South River Falls and then to the bottom of this 83-foot waterfall, the third highest in the park. In spring, wildflowers are plentiful.

Trailhead: Turn left into the South River Picnic Area at Mile 62.8. You'll soon be on a one-way loop road to the right. Not long before completing the loop back to the entrance, watch for the trailhead on your right.

Description: From the trailhead, descend into a hardwood forest. The South River Falls Trail soon crosses the Appalachian Trail (the AT from the left is the return leg of this loop; to the right, the AT leads 0.3 mile to an old road that connects with the Saddleback Mountain Trail, hike 60); continue straight on the South River Falls Trail.

At 0.4 mile the trail swings left into a switchback to the right and descends steeply. After three more switchbacks, you'll see on your right at 0.6

mile the upper part of South River. (A short path to the right leads to the stream's edge.) At 0.7 mile the trail crosses a side creek flowing under the rocks of the trail.

At 1.0 mile, the trail turns right, then left to form an **S** curve; you'll then be closer to the main stream once again. At 1.1 miles, the trail crosses another side stream; rocks cemented together form a stepping-stone bridge over the trickle of water. Ahead you can see the forest opening up where the land drops away at the waterfall.

Continue to a rock bluff that provides your first view of the falls on your right, and then just beyond, at 1.3 miles, you'll reach the overlook for the falls, with a rock wall.

From the overlook, the trail ascends, with a rock bluff on your left, to connect with an old road at 1.5 miles; you'll see a hitching rail on the left. The loop hike continues to the left, but first turn right for a side trip to the bottom of the falls.

You'll descend on the road through a curve to the right that skirts the Rapidan Wildlife Management Area outside the park boundary. The road ends at the South River at 2.0 miles. Then take the rocky footpath that leads upstream to the foot of the waterfall at 2.2 miles. The way can get overgrown with stinging nettle in late summer. The path ends at the plunge pool; above, the waterfall begins as a single stream that separates halfway down to form two falls of water at the bottom. Return the way you came to ascend back to the main loop trail at 2.9 miles. Back at the junction of the South River Falls Trail with the old road, continue straight. (If you're coming from the overlook and did not take the side trip to the bottom of the falls, turn left.)

South River Falls
(Photo by John Amberson, courtesy of Shenandoah National Park)

At 3.3 miles along the loop route, the old road joins the South River Fire Road. These roads have yellow blazes because they are used as horse trails. (To the right, the South River Fire Road reaches the Pocosin Trail, hike 57, in 1.2 miles); turn left up the South River Fire Road to stay on the loop.

Some sections of the fire road are eroded. Ascend along this road until at 4.1 miles the road crosses the AT, which is blazed white (straight ahead, the road reaches Skyline Drive in 0.3 mile; to the right on the AT, you can walk 2.9 miles north to connect with the Pocosin Fire Road—this route can be used for a 7.7-mile loop hike that incorporates the Pocosin Trail, hike 57); turn left on the AT to complete the loop hike.

At 4.6 miles the AT crosses the South River Falls Trail to close the loop. Turn right to return to the trailhead and picnic area at 4.7 miles.

60 | SADDLEBACK MOUNTAIN TRAIL AND AT

Distance: 3.8-mile loop
Difficulty: Moderate
Elevation change: 300 feet
Cautions: Can get overgrown
Connections: AT, South River Falls Trail

Attractions: You'll enjoy an isolated trek through the forest of the Blue Ridge, passing the South River Maintenance Building near a spring and circling Saddleback Mountain. In places the trail can get overgrown because it is seldom used; stinging nettle and briers sometimes crowd the trail.

Trailhead: Turn left into the South River Picnic Area at Mile 62.8. You'll soon be on a one-way loop road to the right. Not long before completing the loop back to the entrance, watch for the the South River Falls trailhead on your right.

Description: From the trailhead, descend on the South River Falls Trail to the crossing of the Appalachian Trail (AT) at a little less than 0.1 mile (to the left, the AT leads north to Big Meadows; straight ahead is the South River Falls Trail, hike 59); turn right on the AT.

After passing through a woods with several large oaks, you'll reach a junction with a service road at 0.3 mile (to the right the service road emerges in 0.1 mile on Skyline Drive at Mile 63.1); bear left here as the AT follows the service road. You'll reach a junction at 0.5 mile (the AT continues to the right toward Swift Run Gap in 2.4 miles); bear left, still on the service road, which now becomes the Saddleback Mountain Trail.

At 0.8 mile, the road arrives at the Potomac Appalachian Trail Club's South River Maintenance Building; no camping is allowed here. To the left just before the structure, you'll see a path to a spring. The Saddleback Mountain Trail continues in front of the building, becoming a moss-covered footpath, although still on an old roadbed. From here on the trail is rocky and sometimes overgrown.

At 1.1 miles, the trail bears right to begin an ascent. You'll pass an old rail fence on the right remaining from an early settlement. The trail descends to cross a shallow stream at 1.8 miles and then reaches a junction with the AT at 1.9 miles (to the left, the AT continues to Swift Run Gap); turn right to complete the loop.

The AT heads uphill to the north, eventually closing the loop when you reach the junction with the beginning of the Saddleback Mountain Trail at the service road at 3.3 miles. Turn left up the service road to the junction at 3.5 miles where the AT turns to the right, and follow it back to the South River Falls Picnic Area at 3.8 miles.

Doyles River Falls

The South District of the park extends from Swift Run Gap to Rockfish Gap at the southern boundary of the park. From Hightop Mountain, you can see almost the entire range of the South District, including Rocky Mount, Rockytop, Rocky Mountain, and Trayfoot and Loft Mountains. Services are available at the Loft Mountain Wayside, Campground, and Picnic Area. The South District is described in two sections: Swift Run Gap to Blackrock and Blackrock to Rockfish Gap.

SWIFT RUN GAP TO BLACKROCK

This northern half of the South District contains several trails that climb the mountain peaks where exposed rock and talus slopes give them names containing the words "rock" or "rocky." Other hikes lead to waterfalls on Doyles River and Jones Run and into the largest watershed in the park, Big Run.

At the Loft Mountain Wayside, you'll find a snack bar, gift shop, gas, rest rooms, and telephone; it's closed in the winter. Across the drive from the wayside, a road leads up the mountain to the Loft Mountain Campground and Picnic Area, which is actually on Big Flat Mountain; Loft Mountain stands just to the north.

Browns Gap, near Blackrock, was named for the Brown family, which once owned much land on the east side of the mountains. Stonewall Jackson's troops camped in Browns Gap for a week during his Civil War Valley Campaign. The Browns Gap Fire Road and Madison Run Fire Road were once a turnpike built through the gap in 1806 following an old trail that had long been used.

Skyline Drive: On US 33 from Swift Run Gap, services and accommodations are available at Elkton to the west and Stanardsville to the east. On Skyline Drive past Swift Run Gap, the parking area for Hightop Mountain (hike 61) is on the right at Mile 66.7. Skyline Drive reaches Swift Run Overlook on the right at Mile 67.2. To the left you can look west to Beldor Ridge and Hanse Mountain in an arm of the park that is across Beldor Hollow. At the Sandy Bottom Overlook on the right at Mile 67.8, look down into Beldor Hollow and the community of Sandy Bottom, with Beldor Ridge and Hanse Mountain beyond.

The Appalachian Trail (AT) crosses the drive at Smith Roach Gap at Mile 68.6; there's parking on the left side (you can follow the AT north 1.8 miles to Hightop Mountain). The Smith Roach Gap Fire Road descends the east side of the mountain to emerge from the park and connect with VA 626 in 1 mile. A spur off this road is the service road for the Hightop Hut.

From the Bacon Hollow Overlook at Mile 69.3 on the left you'll look down Bacon Hollow to a small community. Homes stand below and at the top of Flattop Mountain to the right outside the park. Roundtop Mountain towers over you on the other side of the drive.

At Powell Gap at Mile 69.9 the AT crosses the drive once again; there's parking on the left. From the Eaton Hollow Overlook on the right at Mile 70.6 you'll look down into Eaton Hollow, a branch of Beldor Hollow. To the right stands Bush Mountain and, farther to the right, the obvious rounded top of Roundtop Mountain, the mountain at Bacon Hollow Overlook.

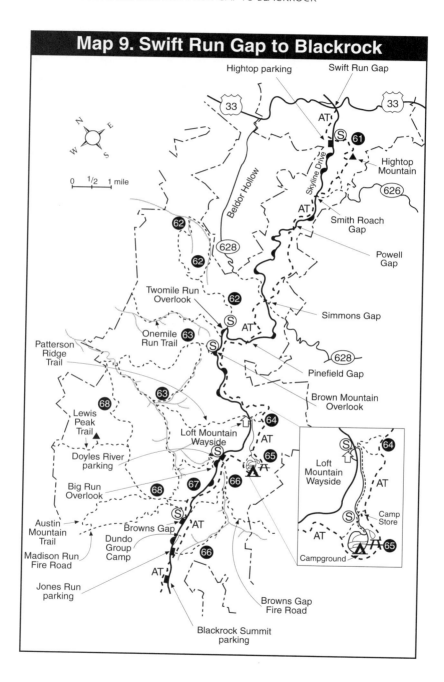

Map 9. Swift Run Gap to Blackrock

Hightop parking

Swift Run Gap

33

33

AT

S 61

Hightop Mountain

626

Beldor Hollow

Skyline Drive

AT

Smith Roach Gap

Powell Gap

62

628

62

Simmons Gap

Twomile Run Overlook

62

S AT

Onemile Run Trail

63

S

628

Patterson Ridge Trail

Pinefield Gap

63

Brown Mountain Overlook

68

Lewis Peak Trail

64

Loft Mountain Wayside

AT

Doyles River parking

65

Big Run Overlook

68 67

66

Austin Mountain Trail

S AT

Browns Gap

Madison Run Fire Road

Dundo Group Camp

66

Jones Run parking

AT

Browns Gap Fire Road

Blackrock Summit parking

S 64

Loft Mountain Wayside

AT

S

Camp Store

AT

65

Campground

The Rocky Mount Overlook on the right at Mile 71.2 offers a good view of Rocky Mount, the mountain with talus slopes straight out from the overlook. Continuing south on the drive, on the left notice the numerous white plumes of goat's beard in June.

From the Beldor Hollow Overlook on the right at Mile 72.2, you'll look into the head of Beldor Hollow to the left. The ridgeline leading to the right to Rocky Mount is the route of the Rocky Mount Trail (hike 62).

At Simmons Gap at Mile 73.2, the AT crosses the drive once again. An old road crosses the gap here also; to the west it descends into Beldor Hollow and to the east it descends into Fork Hollow; outside the park on both sides, the old road becomes VA 628. Just down the road to the east, you'll find the Simmons Gap Ranger Station.

At Mile 74.4 the Loft Mountain Overlook is on the left; you'll look down on Shifflett Hollow below. Loft Mountain stands to the right.

At Mile 75.2 in Pinefield Gap, the AT crosses the drive. Just beyond the crossing, there's graveled parking next to the service road that leads east to the Pinefield Hut on the AT. Just before the Twomile Run Overlook, you can access the Rocky Mount Trail (hike 62).

From the Twomile Run Overlook on the right at Mile 76.2, you'll see Twomile Ridge, with the hollow of Onemile Run on its left and Twomile Run on its right. Farther to the right stands Rocky Mount in the distance. Just beyond the Twomile Run Overlook lies the overgrown trailhead for the Onemile Run Trail, which descends along Onemile Run 3.7 miles to the park boundary; access beyond the boundary is limited.

From the Brown Mountain Overlook on the right at Mile 76.9, you'll have a good view of Rocky Mountain, with the Erwin quartzite cliffs straight out from the overlook. To the left, you can see into the valley of Big Run, with Rockytop Ridge beyond. To the right stands Twomile Ridge and Rocky Mount. From the overlook, you can access the Brown Mountain Trail (hike 63).

The AT passes through the Ivy Creek Overlook, on the left at Mile 77.5. The view east includes Flattop Mountain and Hightop to the left and Loft Mountain to the right.

At the Rockytop Overlook on the right at Mile 78.1, there's a view of the Big Run watershed. To the west you can see Rockytop with talus slopes and, to the right, Brown Mountain and Rocky Mountain. Far to the left stands the peak of Trayfoot Mountain.

The service road to the Ivy Creek Maintenance Hut drops off Skyline Drive to the left at Mile 79.4. On the right side of the drive you'll see the trailhead marker for the Patterson Ridge Trail, which heads out along Patterson Ridge to descend to the Big Run Portal Trail (hike 63) in 3.1 miles. There is no parking here; if you want to hike the Patterson Ridge Trail, continue on to the Loft Mountain Wayside on the right side of Skyline Drive at Mile 79.5, where there is ample parking. On the other side of the drive is the road to the Loft Mountain Campground and Picnic Area, and access to the Frazier Discovery Trail (hike 64) and the Loft Mountain Campground Loop (hike 65).

From the Loft Mountain Wayside, the Doyles River parking area lies on the left side of the road at Mile 81.1, where you can access the Doyles River Trail (hike 66) and the Big Run Loop (hike 67). Just beyond is the Big Run Overlook on the right at Mile 81.2. The overlook offers a panoramic view of the Big Run Valley, which drains 11 square miles, the largest watershed in the park. The low notch in the distant mountains is the Big Run Portal, with Rockytop to the left and Brown and Rocky Mountains to the right.

On the left side of the drive at Mile 81.9, you'll find the Doyles River Overlook. The AT passes through the overlook parking area. The hollow below the overlook is the Doyles River Valley; Jones Run Hollow runs to the right. On the left lies Browns Cove, and the prominent peak outside the park is High Top Mountain (not the Hightop on the AT near Swift Run Gap to the north). The AT crosses the drive at Mile 82.2; there's no parking here.

In Browns Gap at Mile 83.0, the AT crosses the drive again. The Browns Gap Fire Road heads east down the ridge to connect with the Doyles River Trail, and the Madison Run Fire Road is on the west. The Rockytop Trail (hike 68) can be reached off the Madison Run Fire Road.

At Mile 83.7 the Dundo Overlook on the right offers a view to the west; look for blooming mountain laurel in June. Dundo Hollow, containing Madison Run, lies below the overlook, with Furnace Mountain to the left and the peak of Austin Mountain to the right. Farther to the right stands Lewis Mountain and Rockytop Ridge. To the far left stands the peak of Trayfoot Mountain. Also at Mile 83.7 is the turnoff on the left for the Dundo Group Camp; contact the park headquarters for reservations. This was once the site of CCC Camp No. 27.

At Mile 84.1, the Jones Run parking area lies on the left side of the drive. Here you can access the Jones Run Trail (hike 66) for a short walk to Jones Run Falls in 1.7 miles. The AT crosses the drive at Mile 84.3. You'll reach the Blackrock Summit parking area at Mile 84.8.

61 | Hightop via AT

Distance: 1.4 miles one-way
Difficulty: Easy
Elevation gain: 950 feet
Cautions: Rocky sections
Connections: AT

Attractions: The view from near the summit of Hightop, at 3,587 feet the highest peak in the South District, offers a grand introduction to the South

District of the park. Rocky Mount, with exposed rock on its slope, is straight out from the viewpoint. To the left stands Twomile Ridge, Rockytop, and Rocky Mountain. In the foreground, you can see the perfectly rounded summit of Roundtop. Then look for the sharp peak of Trayfoot Mountain on the horizon, with Blackrock to the left, then Loft Mountain, Big Flat Mountain, Little Flat Mountain, Pasture Fence Mountain, Calf Mountain, and Bucks Elbow Mountain.

Trailhead: On the right side of Skyline Drive at Mile 66.7, pull into the parking area for Hightop. The Appalachian Trail crosses the drive at the north end of the parking area (it's 1.2 miles along the AT to the north to Swift Run Gap, where the trail crosses US 33 on the drive overpass); cross Skyline Drive on the AT to the east side of the road.

Description: Follow the AT into the woods. Bear right and begin the ascent of Hightop Mountain. The trail winds up the mountain, with some rocky sections.

After a steep section at 0.9 mile, the trail curves to the right across a level shoulder of the mountain and then curves right again to continue the winding ascent. At 1.3 miles, curve west over another shoulder and then bear left along the edge of the mountain. At rock outcrops, you'll have glimpses to the south; then at 1.4 miles a panoramic view opens of the mountain range to the southwest.

(If you continue south on the AT from the viewpoint, in 100 yards you'll reach a side trail to the left that leads to the summit of Hightop, where a fire lookout tower once stood. On down the AT, you'll pass a spring on the left and descend through masses of purple spiderwort in late spring. At 1.9 miles you'll reach a junction; a trail to the right leads 0.1 mile to the Hightop Hut and a spring; the hut is reserved for long-distance hikers on the Appalachian Trail. Continuing on the AT, you'll cross the service road to the shelter and recross Skyline Drive at Smith Roach Gap at Mile 68.6 in another 1.3 miles.)

62 | ROCKY MOUNT AND GAP RUN TRAILS

Distance: 9.8-mile loop
Difficulty: Moderate
Elevation change: 1,500 feet
Cautions: Steep ascents and descents, creek fords
Connections: None

Attractions: This loop hike explores the peninsula of parkland on the west side of Beldor Hollow. The trail passes through mountain laurel and blueberries. Small trees and bushes can crowd the trail if it has not been cleared recently. Watch for large stands of cinnamon fern.

Trailhead: The Rocky Mount Trail begins on the right at Mile 76.1 on Skyline Drive, but there's no parking at the trailhead, so continue on to the Twomile Run Overlook at Mile 76.2 on the right, where you can park, and walk back up the road 0.1 mile to pick up the trail.

Description: Entering the woods, the Rocky Mount Trail passes over a knoll and heads out along the ridge leading to Rocky Mount. Make a winding descent along the ridge until you level off, and bear left off the ridgeline at 0.6 mile to circle a knoll. Back to the ridgeline at 0.8 mile, swing to the right to circle another knoll.

The trail then makes a long but easy descent to a junction at 2.2 miles (the Gap Run Trail to the right is the return leg of this loop); stay straight to begin the ascent of Rocky Mount.

At 2.4 miles cross a small talus slope and continue a winding ascent with switchbacks and steep sections; the trail passes by large boulders. At 3.0 miles, you'll enter a more open area on the ridgeline, where the trail turns right to continue the ascent. There's a view to the southwest at 3.2 miles, across the hollow of Twomile Run to Twomile Ridge. At 3.3 miles the trail reaches the summit of Rocky Mount, but there's no view here for the trees.

Now descend the northwest side of Rocky Mount. A step down a sheet of rock at 3.5 miles signals a steep section. Swing back to the ridgeline at 3.7 miles and continue the descent.

At 4.3 miles, the trail turns right in the descent, winding down several switchbacks. You'll encounter a small stream, a tributary of Gap Run; follow it down and crisscross the stream at 4.8 miles. The trail turns right once again, descends to a ford of Gap Run, and leads up to a junction at 5.3 miles (an old road to the left, which is the Gap Run Trail, once led to the park boundary in 0.7 mile, but that route is now abandoned); turn right on the road.

The old roadbed becomes rocky before the trail swings off to the right. Upon reaching a clearing, the trail curves left back into the woods. You may hear sounds from the people and vehicles at Beldor Hollow to your left as the trail skirts the park boundary. At 5.5 miles, a trail post stands where there was once a junction, but no more.

Back on the old roadbed, cross runoff from a slough to the left at 5.9 miles. Soon you'll encounter a rocky flood zone along the creek; head straight into the flood zone and turn left to pick up the path.

On the roadbed again, there's a wet area where a drainage runs down the trail for a few yards. At 6.1 miles, the trail turns onto another old road. Rockhop across Gap Run at 6.4 miles. You might encounter a flock of fledgling grouse in early summer; they scatter in all directions while the hen squawks in the undergrowth, trying to draw intruders away.

As the trail gains elevation, the roadbed narrows and becomes eroded. At 6.6 miles, cross Gap Run and continue a winding ascent up the hollow. At 7.0 miles, the trail crosses Gap Run again. You'll continue to ascend, making a steep and rocky climb back to the ridgeline and the junction with the Rocky Mount Trail at 7.6 miles. Now that you've closed the loop, turn left to get back to Skyline Drive in another 2.2 miles.

63 BROWN MOUNTAIN, BIG RUN PORTAL, AND ROCKY MOUNTAIN RUN TRAILS

Distance: 10.1-mile loop
Difficulty: Moderate
Elevation change: 1,625 feet
Cautions: Steep descents and ascents, rocky, creek fords
Connections: Rockytop Trail

Attractions: This interesting loop takes you over the quartzite cliffs of Rocky Mountain and down to the Big Run Portal, where Big Run exits the park through a narrow passage between Brown Mountain on the north and Rockytop to the south. In late May and June, watch for turkeybeard, a clump of white flowers on a tall spike. The trail can get a bit overgrown in summer along Big Run, which you ford numerous times.

Trailhead: Park at the Brown Mountain Overlook on the right at Mile 76.9.

Description: To begin the hike, walk through the gap in the center of the wall at the overlook to pick up the Brown Mountain Trail. The path swings left and right from the overlook. Continue descending to a left turn at

Turkeybeard

Big Run

0.1 mile. The trail then descends out along a ridge with switchbacks to arrive at a junction at 0.7 mile (the Rocky Mountain Run Trail to the left is the return route); stay straight past this junction

Ascend from the saddle along the right side of a knoll. You'll ascend steeply with switchbacks and reach the peak of the knoll at 1.7 miles. Turn right to continue out the ridgeline. You'll reach the crest of Rocky Mountain at 2.3 miles. The trail crosses the top of the white quartzite cliffs you saw from the Brown Mountain Overlook; in fact, you can see the overlook to your left along the crest of the Blue Ridge. Across the exposed rock, the trail turns right over the ridgeline to drop off the ridge and begin a winding descent. The footing is rocky at times.

At 3.2 miles, there's a view from the side of Brown Mountain, the lower peak behind Rocky Mountain; the view is to the southwest with the Big

Run Valley below and the ridge of Rockytop beyond. From Brown Mountain, the trail descends to the west and then rises to another knoll at 3.5 miles with rock outcrops. (Up to the left, a path into rocks along the ridgeline gives a glimpse of the Big Run Valley.)

The trail crosses a talus slope with views of the Bearwallow Run Valley to the north. Continue the winding descent, cross over the ridgeline among exposed rock, and ascend the last knoll on the ridgeline at 4.1 miles. The trail turns steeply off the right side of the knoll to begin a final descent toward Big Run Portal.

The trail switchbacks down the rocky slope of the ridge, passing a small rocky knoll. You'll swing around the end of the ridge at 4.4 miles and continue a steep, winding descent. At 4.9 miles, a good view opens of the Big Run Valley and the talus slopes on the side of Rockytop Ridge. Continuing down the rocky trail, a grand view at 5.1 miles shows the passage of Big Run through the mountains, called the "Big Run Portal."

Curving left, the trail winds down to a junction at 5.3 miles (the makeshift path to the right leads to a camping site on Big Run: this is the approximate origin of a fire in 1986 that burned almost 4,500 acres in the Big Run watershed—you may notice fire-scarred trees in the area); turn left.

Walk a few paces to reach a second junction at an old road that is the Big Run Portal Trail. (To the right, the road crosses a metal bridge over Big Run, a large creek because it drains the largest watershed in the park; the trail then heads down Big Run, where you can glimpse the rock walls of the portal of Big Run through the trees; in 0.5 mile the trail connects with the bottom end of the Rockytop Trail, hike 68, and reaches the park boundary in 0.7 mile—but there's no public access here from outside the park.) To continue this loop hike, head left on the Big Run Portal Trail.

The trail follows the rocky roadbed east up the mountain. At 5.6 miles, ford Big Run to the south side. The trail fords the creek again at 6.0 miles and soon after crosses a side stream. Ford again at 6.4 miles and 6.6 miles. You'll then reach a junction at 6.7 miles. (The Big Run Portal Trail continues straight ahead, up Big Run, fording Rocky Mountain Run to connect with the Patterson Ridge Trail in 0.2 mile and fording Big Run three more times to connect with the Big Run Loop, hike 67, in 2.3 miles.) Turn left on the Rocky Mountain Run Trail to complete this loop hike.

The trail follows an old roadbed to parallel Rocky Mountain Run. At 7.2 miles a rock shelf in the creekbed creates a 3-foot fall of water into a good wading pool for a hot summer day. Ford Rocky Mountain Run at 7.4 miles. By the time you cross again at 8.1 miles, the stream is small enough to rockhop. Soon after, cross back over the stream as you continue up the hollow.

As you ascend, the stream has less and less water until the streambed is dry, unless there have been recent rains. The trail becomes rocky as the hollow narrows and you follow the streambed up. At 9.0 miles, the trail becomes steep in a series of switchbacks that take you up the ridge to the junction with the Brown Mountain Trail to close the loop at 9.4 miles. Turn right to get back to the Brown Mountain Overlook in another 0.7 mile.

64 | FRAZIER DISCOVERY TRAIL

Distance: 1.1-mile loop
Difficulty: Moderate
Elevation change: 500 feet
Cautions: Steep ascent and descent
Connections: AT

Attractions: This trail has one of the finest views in the park and a profusion of blooming phacelia in late May and June. The trail is named for the Frazier family that once lived in the area. The "Discovery" in the trail name means that there is no park interpretation, and so you get to discover what the forest and mountain have to offer.

The trail passes through Patterson Fields, an area where cattle grazed in the early 1900s; the Patterson family drove their cattle from Shenandoah Valley up the route of the Patterson Ridge Trail. Land was cleared for grazing by girdling the trees, which of course caused them to die and allowed light to penetrate to the forest floor; this was called a "deadening." Later, when they had time and needed wood or lumber, the farmers would come back for the standing dead trees. If the trees were never harvested, they would eventually fall and decompose on the ground.

Trailhead: Park at the Loft Mountain Wayside on the right at Mile 79.5.

Description: From the wayside, walk to the north on the sidewalk to cross Skyline Drive to the east side. A few yards up from the drive, the Frazier Discovery Trail begins on the left (the paved path straight ahead continues up the mountain, following the road to the campground). As soon as you turn left on the discovery trail, you'll encounter a fork; take the left fork to hike the loop clockwise.

The trail ascends steeply with switchbacks up to a rock wall at 0.3 mile, where you'll bear right. The trail then turns left to get above the wall and continue the ascent. At 0.4 mile, cross an expanse of bare rock and turn to the right to the rock edge for one of the best views in the park. You're looking west, with Skyline Drive below and Rockytop Ridge in the distance to the left. Below to the right you'll see the Big Run Valley and the portal; farther to the right are Brown Mountain and Rocky Mountain and, far to the right, the peak of Loft Mountain.

The trail bears left from the overlook to a junction with the Appalachian Trail (to the left, the AT passes through a more open area that was once grazing land to a rock outcrop in 0.3 mile with a view east and then continues past the peak of Loft Mountain in 0.7 mile before beginning a descent toward Ivy Creek Spring); to continue on the Frazier Discovery Trail Loop, turn right on the AT.

In June, masses of pale blue phacelia line the trail, making it a beautiful walk. You'll soon pass a path up to a rock outcrop and another view west, virtually the same view as the previous viewpoint on the discovery trail. At 0.5 mile there's another junction (the AT continues straight ahead to descend through a gap and then ascend to the Loft Mountain Campground on Big Flat Mountain in 1.3 miles); turn right on the Frazier Discovery Trail.

You'll make a steep descent through the open area that was once Patterson Fields; the small trees in this area are evidence that the land was once cleared. The trail reenters more mature forest and continues a descent to close the loop at 1.1 miles. Turn left to reach the paved path, then turn right on the paved path to recross Skyline Drive and return to the Loft Mountain Wayside.

65 | LOFT MOUNTAIN CAMPGROUND LOOP

Distance: 1.6 miles
Difficulty: Easy
Elevation change: 100 feet
Cautions: None
Connections: AT

Attractions: If you're staying at Loft Mountain Campground, this hike along a section of the Appalachian Trail (AT) offers a pleasant walk with sunset views after you've set up camp.

Trailhead: Across from the Loft Mountain Wayside on the right at Mile 79.5, turn left onto the road that leads to the campground on Big Flat Mountain. After you pass the turnoff to the left to the campground store (which has food and showers for campers), turn into the parking area on the right for the amphitheater. (There are also several access points from the campground area to this loop trail.)

Description: Walk down the paved path that leads to the amphitheater for a few paces and turn left on a grassy trail that's the beginning of the loop. At 0.1 mile you'll reach a junction with the AT (to the right it heads south to Browns Gap in 3.0 miles); turn left on the AT to circle the campground.

The AT makes some short, steep ascents to get on a level with the campground and reach a junction at 0.3 mile. (To the left, you can walk for 0.1 mile to reach the campground at campsite A-8; to the right, you can walk down to an overlook that offers a good location to watch the sunset, with Blackrock and Trayfoot Mountains to the south.) Continue straight ahead.

At 0.5 mile, the trail skirts the back of the campground near campsite A-14, where it's another short walk to the left up to the campground; on the AT here you'll find views to the southwest, another good spot for watching the day end.

Continue around the campground through a forest thick with fern to a side trail to the left at 0.8 mile (another access from the campground to the AT). At 0.9 mile you'll pass some paths on the left that lead up to the picnic area.

The trail then heads downhill to reach a junction at 1.4 miles (the AT continues straight to eventually link with the Frazier Discovery Trail, hike 64, in 1.0 mile); turn left on a trail that leads up to the camp store.

Ascend steeply to the store, where an expanse of grass offers a view to the east. Pick up the paved walk that passes beside the store. Out front, you'll connect at 1.5 miles with the paved path that leads down from the campground (to the right, it leads to the wayside); turn left up the paved path to pass in front of the store, cross the campground road, and return to the amphitheater parking at 1.6 miles.

66 | DOYLES RIVER TRAIL, JONES RUN TRAIL, AND AT

Distance: 7.8-mile loop
Difficulty: Moderate
Elevation change: 1,400 feet
Cautions: Stream fords, steep sections, highway crossings
Connections: AT, Browns Gap Fire Road, Madison Run Fire Road, Big Run Loop

Attractions: This favorite hike includes the upper and lower Doyles River Falls and Jones Run Falls. The large tulip poplar trees, cascading streams, waterfalls, and oodles of wildflowers make this a perfect hike on a sunny spring day.

Trailhead: Pull into the Doyles River parking area at Mile 81.1 on the left side of Skyline Drive. The trailhead is at the far right of the parking area.

Description: The trail descends, crossing the Appalachian Trail (to the right the AT is the return route for this loop hike; to the left the AT leads 1.2 miles north to the Loft Mountain Campground); continue straight ahead, downhill on the Doyles River Trail.

You'll pass a spring on the left at 0.3 mile and soon after reach a fork (a side trail left leads up to the Doyles River Cabin, which may be rented from

Jones Run Falls

the Potomac Appalachian Trail Club); to continue on the Doyles River Trail, take the right fork.

At 0.5 mile, cross a creek on stepping stones. You'll step over a small creek at 0.8 mile that's probably dry in summer and soon parallel Doyles River on the right, a small stream at this point. The trail crosses Browns Gap Fire Road at 0.9 mile. (To the right, the road crosses Doyles River on a metal bridge and ascends to Skyline Drive in 1.8 miles at Browns Gap at

Mile 83.0. To the left the road descends the mountain to emerge from the park in 1.5 miles and become VA 629.) Stay straight on the Doyles River Trail.

You soon cross Doyles River on stones; continue down along the river to pass a small drop and then reach the head of the upper falls of the Doyles River at 1.2 miles. On down the trail, you'll swing right and left, rockhop a small stream, and reach a junction (a side trail to the left leads to the bottom of this upper falls, a two-step cascade of water 28 feet high; notice the large tulip poplars nearby); continue straight down the trail.

There's a rock wall on the right that in late May is covered in pale blue phacelia. Passing the wall, you'll switchback left and descend to the lower falls of the Doyles River at 1.5 miles, a 63-foot cascade of water.

The trail switchbacks to the right at a view of the falls and continues to descend along Doyles River, which contains more cascades and spillways. At 1.7 miles, you cross a bridge over a steeply cascading stream that's a tributary of the river. Watch for a huge tulip poplar beside the trail at 2.0 miles. At 2.1 miles the Doyles River Trail ends at a junction with the Jones Run Trail; turn to the right up along Jones Run.

At 2.2 miles the trail fords Jones Run and continues upstream. Notice the large poplars and oaks along this stretch. The trail ascends more steeply and becomes rocky at 2.6 miles. You'll cross a side stream on rocks. Notice a nice water slide in Jones Run on the way up. At 2.8 miles the trail reaches Jones Run Falls, a 42-foot drop that's part cascade, part waterfall.

Switchback left at the bottom of the falls to continue ascending the trail. Up past massive blocks of stone, switchback right to get above the falls (an unofficial side path to the right leads to the top of the falls; take care).

The main trail continues to ascend along Jones Run through patches of wild geranium in late spring, passing big trees and big rocks. At 3.2 miles, watch for where Jones Run breaks into a multitude of rivulets among rocks in the streambed (soon after, a side path to the right leads to a pool in the stream where you can take a rest with your feet in the water).

The main trail ascends more steeply and then levels off to swing right; rockhop the upper part of Jones Run at 4.0 miles. Ascending again, the trail switchbacks left at 4.2 miles and crosses the trace of a road that's the right-of-way for the waterline to the nearby Dundo Group Camp. At 4.5 miles you'll reach a junction with the Appalachian Trail at the Jones Run parking area at Mile 84.1 on Skyline Drive (to the left, the AT leads south 1.3 miles to Blackrock); turn right on the AT to complete this loop hike.

At 5.1 miles the AT skirts the backside of the Dundo Group Camp (a path to the left leads up to the camp); stay straight on the AT to descend into Browns Gap, at Mile 83.0 on Skyline Drive, at 5.7 miles. Cross the drive to the right and enter the parking area for the Madison Run Fire Road on the west side of the drive. Notice that, on the east side of the drive, the Browns Gap Fire Road has ascended to here from the Doyles River Trail.

Follow the AT where it turns up to the right from the Madison Run Fire Road parking area. The trail ascends a dry south-facing slope with laurel, oaks, and blueberry bushes. At 6.3 miles, you reach a junction (the Big Run Loop, hike 67, is to the left); stay straight on the AT.

Descend to cross Skyline Drive to the left at 6.6 miles. Now on the east side of the drive, the trail drops to the right of a rock outcrop. At 6.8 miles, the AT emerges at the Doyles River Overlook at Mile 81.9 on Skyline Drive. Walk straight through the overlook parking area and pick up the trail again at the far back corner of the parking lot.

Back into the woods, the AT continues to parallel the drive until it reaches a junction with the Doyles River Trail at 7.8 miles, closing the loop below the Doyles River parking area. Turn left up the trail to get back to your starting point.

 67 | Big Run Loop

Distance: 5.8 miles
Difficulty: Easy
Elevation change: 1,100 feet
Cautions: Stream crossings
Connections: Big Run Portal Trail, Rockytop Trail, Madison Run Spur Trail, AT, Doyles River Trail

Attractions: Flowering bushes line this hike into the Big Run watershed. You'll pass through pinxter-flower and deerberry blooming in spring and laurel blooming in early summer as you hike through the upper watershed of the Big Run Valley.

Trailhead: The Big Run Loop trail begins at the Big Run Overlook on the right at Mile 81.2. There's better parking at the Doyles River parking area on the left at Mile 81.1, and since the loop passes through that parking area, begin your hike there.

Description: From the parking area, walk south on Skyline Drive and cross to the Big Run Overlook on the west side at 0.1 mile; take care along the highway. At the overlook, walk through the gap in the rock wall and pick up the Big Run Loop, which descends to the left.

At 0.3 mile, the trail switchbacks right in the descent. In a saddle at 0.7 mile between the main Blue Ridge and a small knoll to the west, the trail curves back left in the descent. You'll soon round the head of a hollow and cross a tributary of Big Run at 1.2 miles. Watch for plenty of crested dwarf iris through this section.

The trail then heads out along a ridge between the tributary and Big Run. At 1.8 miles the trail curves left off the ridge and descends to a rockhop crossing of Big Run at 2.2 miles; notice to the left the two streams that converge to create Big Run. Switchback to the right up from the creek to a junction at 2.3 miles. (The Big Run Portal Trail, part of hike 63, is to the right; down that trail, it's 2.1 miles to the Patterson Ridge Trail, 2.3 miles to the Rocky Mountain Run Trail, 3.7 miles to the Brown Mountain Trail, and 4.2 miles to a junction with the Rockytop Trail, hike 68—several loop hikes can be made using these trails.) Turn left at this junction to stay on the Big Run Loop.

Along the trail are standing dead oak trees, killed by gypsy moth caterpillars. Ascending, switchback left at 2.4 miles and right at 3.2 miles. The trail continues by curving left to a four-way junction at 3.6 miles. (The Rockytop Trail, hike 68, leads to the right to pass the Austin Mountain Trail and Lewis Peak Trail, and connect with the Big Run Portal Trail in 5.7 miles; straight ahead, the Madison Run Spur Trail leads 0.3 mile to Madison Run Fire Road.) Turn left up along the ridge to continue on the Big Run Loop trail.

You'll reach a junction with the Appalachian Trail at 4.3 miles (to the right, the AT leads to Browns Gap); turn left on the AT to complete the loop.

Descend to cross Skyline Drive to the left at 4.6 miles. Now on the east side of the drive, the trail drops to the right of a rock outcrop. At 4.8 miles, the AT emerges at the Doyles River Overlook, at Mile 81.9 on Skyline Drive. Walk straight through the overlook parking area and pick up the trail again at the far back corner of the parking lot.

Back into the woods, the AT continues to parallel the drive until it reaches a junction at 5.8 miles, below the Doyles River parking area (straight ahead, the AT continues on to Loft Mountain); turn left up the Doyles River Trail to get back to your starting point.

68 | ROCKYTOP TRAIL

Distance: 6.8 miles one-way; views from Rockytop, 4.6 miles one-way
Difficulty: Moderate
Elevation loss: 1,500 feet
Cautions: Talus slope crossings, long descent
Connections: Big Run Loop, Austin Mountain Trail, Lewis Peak Trail, Big Run Portal Trail

Attractions: Out along Rockytop Ridge, you'll have fine views to the southwest from talus fields along the slope of the mountain. The hike ends at the Big Run Portal, where you can turn up the Big Run Portal Trail to make a loop back to Browns Gap.

Trailhead: In Browns Gap at Mile 83.0, turn in at a parking area on the right, at the beginning of Madison Run Fire Road. Head down the Madison Run Fire Road, which is blocked to vehicles by a chain. (For a little longer access, head north from the parking area on the Appalachian Trail (AT), which connects with the Big Run Loop, hike 67, where you turn left to reach the beginning of the Rockytop Trail in a total of 1.3 miles.)

Description: In 0.8 mile, where Madison Run Fire Road curves right, there's a junction (the fire road continues straight ahead, down the mountain, to emerge from the park as VA 663 in 4.3 miles); turn right onto the Madison Run Spur Trail.

The spur trail ascends to a four-way junction at 1.1 miles (the Big Run Loop, hike 67, straight ahead leads to Big Run and to the right leads to the AT); turn left on the Rockytop Trail.

Ascend over a knoll and then another. The trail descends to a junction at 1.5 miles (the Austin Mountain Trail to the left runs southwest over Austin Mountain and descends to a junction with the Madison Run Fire Road in 3.2 miles); bear right to continue on the Rockytop Trail.

Out along Rockytop Ridge, the trail eventually reaches a junction at 3.3 miles. (The Lewis Peak Trail to the left heads west past Lewis Peak and descends to the park boundary in 2.6 miles; there's no access from outside the park. At Lewis Peak, a side trail leads to the summit for a view west.) Bear right at this junction with the Lewis Peak Trail.

The Rockytop Trail heads down a rocky slope, soon turns right in a long descent, and then begins an ascent of the peak of Rockytop. You'll cross a talus slope at 3.7 miles that offers a view of Big Run Valley to the right and the Lewis Run Hollow to the left. To the far left stands Lewis Peak. Straight ahead is the next peak along Rockytop Ridge.

The trail makes a long descent from Rockytop, with the next peak looming before you at 2,856 feet. In fact, this next peak is a couple of hundred feet higher than the one called Rockytop that you've just covered. From the saddle between the two peaks, ascend the left side of the second peak. The trail crosses talus slopes. At 4.6 miles, cross a wide talus slope offering a view across Lewis Run Hollow to Lewis Peak and, to the left, Lewis Mountain and Austin Mountain—a different Lewis Mountain from the one in the Central District.

After circling this second peak along Rockytop Ridge, you'll begin an ascent with switchbacks to reach the ridgeline at 4.8 miles. The trail then descends, eventually dropping off the ridge in switchbacks to reach a junction with the Big Run Portal Trail (hike 63) at 6.8 miles. (From here you can turn right to ascend on the Big Run Portal Trail for 4.2 miles to the Big Run Loop, hike 67, and turn right for another 2.4 miles to return to Browns Gap; this is a loop hike of 13.4 miles total.)

BLACKROCK TO ROCKFISH GAP

This southernmost section of the park includes Blackrock, Trayfoot Mountain, Calvary Rocks, and Turk Mountain. In addition to traveling these mountain peaks, hikes descend along Paine Run to the site of the Blackrock Springs Hotel and down Cold Spring Hollow into Riprap Hollow.

East of Turk Gap, the Charlottesville reservoir lies on the Moormans River, where the North and South Forks come together. The Moorman family settled land in the area of the river in the early 1700s. West of Turk Gap, at the community of Crimora, mining for manganese began in the 1860s and continued off and on until 1946; the manganese was used with iron in making steel. During World War II, the Crimora Mine produced more manganese than any other mining operation in the United States. The mine is thought to be named after a young woman.

The South District ends at Rockfish Gap. An early road through Rockfish Gap became a turnpike in 1808; Mountain Top Hotel and Leakes Tavern were located in the gap along the road. Now I-64 and US 250 pass through the gap. Services and accommodations are available in Waynesboro to the west and Charlottesville to the east.

Skyline Drive: The Blackrock Summit parking area is on the right at Mile 84.8; you can access the Blackrock Summit Loop (hike 69), the Trayfoot Mountain Trail (hike 70), and Furnace Mountain Trail (hike 71). From the Trayfoot Mountain Overlook on the left at Mile 86.8, you can look east down a hollow to the North Fork of the Moormans River. Far to the right, you can see west over Blackrock Gap to the Shenandoah Valley.

The Appalachian Trail (AT) crosses Skyline Drive at Mile 87.2. Then the drive passes through Blackrock Gap at Mile 87.4, where you can access the Paine Run Trail (hike 72).

At the Horsehead Mountain Overlook on the right at Mile 88.6, you can look across Paine Run Hollow, with Horsehead Mountain beyond and Buzzard Rock in the distance. The closer peak to the left is Calvary Rocks, and Trayfoot Mountain stands to the right. On the left side of the drive, phyllite and sandstone of the Hampton Formation are visible in the rock wall. The AT crosses the drive at Mile 88.9.

The Riprap parking area lies on the right at Mile 90.0, where you can pick up the AT to reach the Riprap Trail (hike 73). From the Riprap Hollow Overlook on the right at Mile 91.4, you can view Riprap Hollow, with Wildcat Ridge to the left.

At the Moormans River Overlook on the left at Mile 92.0, you can see the reservoir for Charlottesville to the southeast. Parking for the Wildcat

Map 10. Blackrock to Rockfish Gap

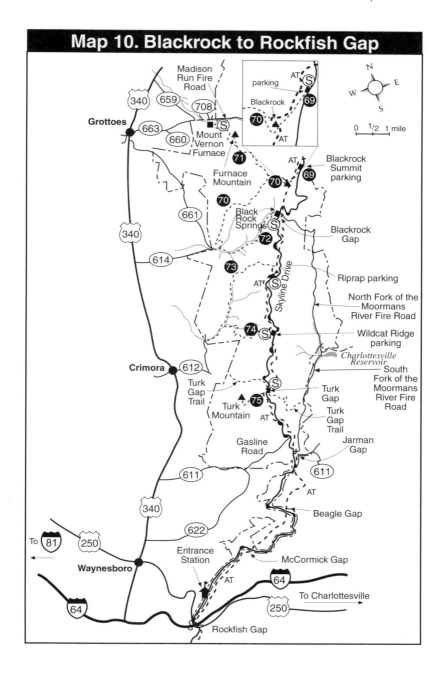

Ridge Trail (hike 74) lies on the right at Mile 92.1. At Mile 92.4, the AT crosses Skyline Drive; there's parking on the right side.

At Crimora Lake Overlook on the right at Mile 92.6, there's a view west, with Turk Mountain to the far left and Wildcat Ridge to the right in front of Rocks Mountain. Down from the overlook, you can look toward the community of Crimora and two lakes associated with the mining operation. Crimora Lake lies directly out from the overlook in among trees; it's hard to spot because the water is black, but maybe you'll catch the sun shining on the water surface. A small stream was dammed to create the lake in 1915 to supply water for washing mining ore. To the left, you'll see a blue-green lake that is a water-filled mine pit.

At the Turk Mountain Overlook on the right at Mile 93.7, you can look southwest to Turk Mountain, where exposed Erwin quartzite makes a slash across the top of the mountain; it looks like a roadcut, but it is a natural feature. Skyline Drive passes through Turk Gap at Mile 94.1, where you can access the Turk Mountain Trail (hike 75).

The AT crosses the drive at the north end of the Sawmill Run Overlook, on the right side of Skyline Drive at Mile 95.3. Sawmill Run lies below the overlook, with the two summits of Calf Mountain to the left and Sawmill Ridge and Turk Mountain to the right.

You'll have virtually the same view from the Sawmill Ridge Overlook on the right at Mile 95.9. Across the drive, there's a good exposure of the sandstone, quartzite, and phyllite of the Weverton Formation, mostly rust-colored from iron deposits.

At Mile 96.1, Gasline Road descends from Skyline Drive down the west side of the mountain to emerge from the park and connect with VA 611/622. The road was built for a gas pipeline; access is limited.

The drive passes through Jarman Gap at Mile 96.8; Thomas Jarman owned the gap in the early 1800s. Here you can access the AT by roads on the east. To the left, the South Fork of the Moormans River Fire Road heads north toward the Charlottesville Reservoir. To the right, the Bucks Elbow Road branches at the park boundary; the left branch heads up Bucks Elbow Mountain to a radio tower, and the right branch continues down the mountain as VA 611.

From Jarman Gap south, the park boundary is not much more than the width of Skyline Drive; the AT mostly travels outside the park, reentering occasionally to cross the drive. The park once ended at Jarman Gap but in 1961 was extended south to Rockfish Gap. From Jarman Gap, the AT heads south to leave the park and reach the Potomac Appalachian Trail Club's Calf Mountain Hut in 1.0 mile and the summit of Calf Mountain in 1.6 miles.

At the Calf Mountain Overlook on the right at Mile 98.9, you can see Waynesboro below, with Scott and Bear Den Mountains to the left and Sawmill Ridge and Turk Mountain to the right.

The AT crosses the drive in Beagle Gap at Mile 99.5; to the north it's a mile to the summit of Calf Mountain. From the Beagle Gap Overlook on the left at Mile 99.8, Greenwood Hollow leads to the Piedmont on the east.

The AT crosses the drive in McCormick Gap at Mile 102.1. Below McCormick Gap Overlook on the right at Mile 102.4 lies Sawmill Run valley, with Sawmill Ridge on the left. The nearby mountain on the right with the radio towers is Bear Den Mountain.

At Mile 104.6 stands the Rockfish Gap Entrance Station. The AT comes down from the east to join the drive at Mile 105.2 and stays on the road to cross US 250 and I-64 in Rockfish Gap at Mile 105.4. Below, a railroad tunnel runs through the mountain. In Rockfish Gap, you leave Shenandoah National Park. Although Skyline Drive ends, the scenic highway continues south as the Blue Ridge Parkway for 469 miles to Great Smoky Mountains National Park.

69 | BLACKROCK SUMMIT LOOP

Distance: 1.0 mile
Difficulty: Easy
Elevation change: 200 feet
Cautions: Talus slopes
Connections: Trayfoot Mountain Trail, AT, Blackrock Spur Trail

Attractions: Outstanding views circle the summit of Blackrock. Take care if you climb the peak for a wider view; it's a difficult rock scramble. The rock's gray appearance is due to rock tripe, a lichen that grows on the rock. (There's also a Blackrock in the Central District near the Big Meadows Lodge.)

Trailhead: On the right side of Skyline Drive, turn in at the Blackrock Summit parking area at Mile 84.8.

Description: Take the Trayfoot Mountain Trail (hike 70), on the left of the parking area, where it follows an old road uphill. You'll ascend steeply to a place at 0.1 mile where the trail touches the Appalachian Trail on the right (the AT to the right passes just below the parking area). The Trayfoot Mountain Trail bypasses Blackrock Summit, and so you must step over onto the AT to go left and continue ascending.

At 0.5 mile, the trail emerges at Blackrock, a huge jumble of boulders forming a mountain peak; a talus slope to the right offers a view northwest to Madison Run in Dundo Hollow.

The AT circles the summit of Blackrock to a junction (the Blackrock Spur Trail to the right leads 0.1 mile down to a junction with the Trayfoot Mountain Trail, hike 70); continue to the left on the AT, circling the summit for views to the southwest down Paine Run Hollow.

View from Blackrock Summit

You'll reenter the woods and reach a junction at 0.6 mile where the AT crosses an old road that is the Trayfoot Mountain Trail. (To the right, it circles below Blackrock Summit; straight ahead, the AT continues toward the Blackrock Hut in 0.5 mile and Blackrock Gap in 1.1 miles.) Turn left on the Trayfoot Mountain Trail to return to the Blackrock Summit parking area at 1.0 mile.

70 | TRAYFOOT MOUNTAIN TRAIL

Distance: 5.4 miles one-way
Difficulty: Moderate
Elevation loss: 1,950 feet
Cautions: Overgrown in places
Connections: AT, Blackrock Spur Trail, Furnace Mountain
Trail, Paine Run Trail

Attractions: You'll cross the summit of Trayfoot Mountain and have a good view of Buzzard Rock Mountain. The odd name of Trayfoot Mountain came from the footprints of a bear; a hunter tracking the animal across the mountain said the paw prints were nearly as big as a "dough-tray." There are plenty of wildflowers in spring along the trail, but it can get overgrown in summer.

Trailhead: Begin at the Blackrock Summit parking area on the right at Mile 84.8.

Description: The Trayfoot Mountain Trail begins at the left side of the parking area, where it follows an old road uphill. At 0.1 mile, you'll reach a junction of sorts where the Appalachian Trail skirts the road on the right (to the left it leads to the summit of Blackrock in 0.4 mile; to the right it heads back to the parking area); continue straight on the Trayfoot Mountain Trail.

At 0.4 mile, there's another junction with the AT (to the left, the AT leads toward the Blackrock Hut in 0.5 mile and Blackrock Gap in 1.1 miles; to the right, the AT leads around Blackrock Summit); stay straight on the old road, which now descends as it circles below Blackrock.

In 100 yards you'll pass another old road on the left (it leads back toward the AT); stay straight on the Trayfoot Mountain Trail. Cross a talus slope

Buzzard Rock

below Blackrock and ascend to a junction at 0.6 mile (the Blackrock Spur Trail on the right leads 0.1 mile up to the AT on Blackrock Summit); stay straight on the old road as it descends.

The trail drops through a sag in the ridge and continues uphill. You'll reach a junction at 1.4 miles (to the right the Furnace Mountain Trail, hike 71, leads out along the ridge to the Furnace Mountain summit and then descends to Madison Run in 3.4 miles); stay on the Trayfoot Mountain Trail, which curves left and continues ascending.

You reach the summit of Trayfoot Mountain at 1.6 miles. The trail now heads out along the ridgeline, where you'll have occasional views of Paine Run Hollow below. As you follow the ridgeline, the trail first heads west and then south in a big curve that you hardly notice. The trail has some ups and downs along the ridge and is lined with a thick covering of grass. In some steeper sections, the trail switchbacks in the descent. You pass rocky knolls and lichen-covered blocks of stone along the ridgeline.

At 4.6 miles the trail reaches a point of the ridge that offers a view west out to farmland of the Shenandoah Valley and left across Paine Run to Buzzard Rock, a perfect cone-shaped mountain from this perspective. The trail swings left past rock outcrops to descend off the ridge. You can look across Lefthand Hollow to Horsehead Mountain, and then the trail switchbacks right in the descent, dropping to end at a junction with the Paine Run Trail (hike 72) at 5.4 miles.

(To the right, the Paine Run Trail leads 0.3 mile to the park boundary. To the left, the trail heads up Paine Run to reach Skyline Drive at Blackrock Gap in 3.4 miles. You can pick up the AT there to make a circuit hike back to the Trayfoot Mountain Trail for a total loop of 9.9 miles and back to Blackrock Parking at 10.3 miles.)

71 | FURNACE MOUNTAIN SUMMIT

Distance: 2.2 miles one-way
Difficulty: Moderate
Elevation gain: 2,000 feet
Cautions: Creek ford, long ascent
Connections: Madison Run Fire Road, Trayfoot Mountain Trail

Attractions: Furnace Mountain's summit offers a great view to the north. On the western park boundary, the remains of the Mount Vernon Furnace, for which the mountain is named, can still be found. The furnace was built around 1830 and operated until the Civil War and only sporadically afterward. The entire operation included an office building, the super-intendent's house, and cabins for the workers. The iron ore was hauled from six mines in the area. The furnace chamber was filled with ore, lime-stone for removing impurities, and charcoal for the fire. Carbon monoxide from the burning charcoal combined with oxygen in the ore to leave pure iron. The molten iron flowed out into holes dug in the surrounding sand and solidified into pigs of iron, which were then hauled to a foundry at Port Republic.

Trailhead: The Mount Vernon Furnace lies on the park's western bound-ary, so for a shorter route to the summit and to see the furnace, start on that end. To reach the western end of the trail, you must leave the park at Swift Run Gap on US 33 or at Rockfish Gap on US 250, then drive east to US 340, and travel to the town of Grottoes. In Grottoes, turn east on VA 663. You'll pass VA 660 on the right at 1.2 miles and VA 659 on the left at 2.2 miles. The road crosses Madison Run and then passes a gravel road to the left at 2.5 miles. Watch for two houses on the left at 2.6 miles; the Mount Vernon Fur-nace stands in the woods across the creek on your right just past the sec-ond house. Continue driving straight ahead to pass a gravel road to the left at 2.7 miles that is VA 708. Then at 2.8 miles you'll find a dirt road to the left at a wide place in the road, where you can pull over on the right and park. Do not drive any farther up the road, because there's no place to turn around. From where you parked, you can walk back up the road to the furnace, where you can glimpse it through the trees. With leaves on the trees, you'll have trouble seeing the furnace, a pyramid of large blocks of stone, used for smelting iron. Only at low water should you cross the creek to get to it.

(To get to the eastern end of the Furnace Mountain Trail, from Skyline Drive at the Blackrock Summit parking area on the right at Mile 84.8, walk 1.4 miles along the Trayfoot Mountain Trail, hike 70.)

Description: To walk the Furnace Mountain Trail, continue up the road from the parking space near the furnace. At 0.1 mile, pass around a chain gate to enter the park, where the road becomes the Madison Run Fire Road. Soon after, you reach a junction (the Madison Run Fire Road continues straight to ascend the ridge and emerge on Skyline Drive in 5.0 miles at Browns Gap); turn right on the Furnace Mountain Trail.

Ford Madison Run at 0.2 mile. The trail then turns right and soon be-gins an ascent of Furnace Mountain in a broad curve to the left. Along the traverse of the south-facing slope of the mountain, you'll see a profusion of mountain laurel and frequent blueberry.

At 1.0 mile, the trail curves to the right, through the head of a hollow, and continues ascending. Swing around the side of the mountain to the left at 1.4 miles, where you'll see ahead a saddle between two peaks of Furnace Mountain. The trail crosses a talus slope and ascends to the saddle and a junction at 1.7 miles. Take the 0.5-mile side trail to the left that leads up through rocks and across talus slopes over the summit of Furnace Mountain at 2.2 miles, and steeply down to a rock outcrop that offers a view to the north. You'll see Austin Mountain to the left and its long ridge running up to the Blue Ridge. Rockytop stands at a distance in the center of the view, and between Rockytop and Austin, Lewis Mountain just peeks over the shoulder of Austin Mountain.

(From the junction, the Furnace Mountain Trail continues straight ahead to ascend the right-hand peak and continue up the ridge, passing over two more knolls along the way, eventually connecting with the Trayfoot Mountain Trail, hike 70, on Trayfoot Mountain in another 1.7 miles.)

72 | PAINE RUN TRAIL

Distance: 3.7 miles one-way; Black Rock Springs, 1.1 miles one-way
Difficulty: Easy; strenuous exploring hotel site
Elevation loss: 900 feet
Cautions: Creek crossings
Connections: AT, North Fork of the Moormans River Fire Road, Trayfoot Mountain Trail

Attractions: The site of the Black Rock Springs Hotel can still be found on a side path as you descend the mountain. There was a hotel of some sort at this site as early as 1835, fifty-three years before George F. Pollock held his first camp on Stony Man Mountain. The Black Rock Springs Hotel served as a summer retreat for visitors from coastal Virginia, Baltimore, and Philadelphia. The resort had various owners and changed much over the years. It was taken over by the Black Rock Springs Improvement Company in the 1880s and reached its peak with two rows of cottages curving around a three-story hotel. There were seven springs touted as curing various ailments. A fire in 1909 swept through the forest, taking the hotel and cottages with it. A nearby boarding house was not destroyed, and it later became known as the Black Rock Springs Hotel, which survived until the park was established.

Trailhead: In Blackrock Gap at Mile 87.4, park on the right side of the drive. On the left side of the drive, you'll see a fire road that descends to the North Fork of the Moormans River outside the park; that road then reenters the park and heads south toward the Charlottesville Reservoir; the lower portion of the road was damaged in a 1995 flood and has since been reconstructed as a horse trail. The old road that ascended from the North Fork and crossed the mountain through Blackrock Gap is now the Paine Run Trail on the west side of the mountain. (The AT passes by on the left side of the drive, so if you're walking a loop with the Trayfoot Mountain Trail, hike 70, and up the Paine Run Trail, cross the drive here to get on the AT and head north back to the Trayfoot Mountain Trail in 1.3 miles.)

Description: From where you parked, follow the old road down the west side of the mountain. At 0.6 mile, the road curves right in the descent. Then at 1.0 mile, the road curves back left. In this second curve, you'll see the trace of a road heading off to

Blackrock Springs

the right. This old road once led to the Black Rock Springs Hotel. (You can explore this area, although the going can get a little rough because the way is no longer maintained. The path following the roadbed gets overgrown, and trees have fallen across the trail. About 0.1 mile in, you'll find some foundations and a walled-in spring.)

Continuing down the old road that's the Paine Run Trail, you'll see across Paine Run Hollow to Horsehead Mountain on your right. As you parallel Paine Run, cross small drainages that flow toward the creek. At 2.8 miles, cross Paine Run to the right. Sometimes the creekbed is dry at this location, with the water flowing under the rocks; sometimes you'll have to ford. Continue down the run, which at the lower elevations has nice pools and spillways.

Cross the stream that flows out of Lefthand Hollow and reach a junction at 3.4 miles (the Trayfoot Mountain Trail, hike 70, is to the right; the Paine Run Trail, the Trayfoot Mountain Trail, and the AT make a good 9.9-mile loop hike); stay left on the Paine Run Trail.

The trail continues down the old road, crossing the run two more times and reaching the park boundary at 3.7 miles. The trail emerges from the park at a junction of VA 661 and VA 614; there's access from outside the park only on VA 661.

73 | Riprap Trail

**Distance: 4.9 miles one-way; Calvary Rocks,
1.4 miles one-way**
Difficulty: Moderate
Elevation loss: 1,300 feet
Cautions: Rock bluffs, stream fords
Connections: AT, Wildcat Ridge Trail

Attractions: You'll have views from Calvary Rocks and Chimney Rock, and at the lower end in June, Catawba rhododendron bloom rose-purple; this rhododendron is frequent in the Blue Ridge to the south, but only grows at lower elevations this far north. Be aware that fires in 1998 and 1999 burned the undergrowth in this part of the South District.

Trailhead: Pull into the Riprap parking area at Mile 90.0 on the right side of Skyline Drive.

Description: At the end of the parking area, take the short path that ascends to the Appalachian Trail (AT). Turn right on the AT and ascend through azalea and mountain laurel to a junction at 0.4 mile (straight ahead the AT continues north to Blackrock Gap in 2.2 miles); turn left down the Riprap Trail.

The trail curves right on a long descent into a sag, and then ascends over a knoll at 0.9 mile. Down again, curving left and right, you'll drop through a saddle and then ascend over another knoll at 1.2 miles. The trail then descends into another sag among exposed rock that looks similar to riprap, rock that's thrown down to shore up a slope and prevent erosion.

Ascend for a third time, toward the left and up to the ridgeline at Calvary Rocks at 1.4 miles. (A side path to the right takes you out to the rock bluff with a view to the northwest across Paine Run to Horsehead Mountain.) The main trail continues out along the rocky ridge, through a field of boulders standing on end at 1.5 miles, and finally to another side path on the right at 1.6 miles that leads out to a view northwest. Chimney Rock stands just out from the viewpoint. Iron pegs in the rocks once held a small bridge to the top of Chimney Rock.

The trail curves left at Chimney Rock and descends through laurel to once more reach the edge of the mountain at 2.0 miles for another view across Paine Run Hollow, with Buzzard Rock to the left. Soon after, the trail begins a descent off the ridge into Cold Spring Hollow. At 2.4 miles, the trail swings right in the descent. As you continue down, watch for a rock beside the trail with a tree growing on top that makes a good spot for lunch. Notice the huge oak on the left past the rock bench.

At first, the streambed in Cold Spring Hollow is dry, with the water running under the rocks in dry seasons. But as you descend farther, the water emerges and tall cinnamon ferns stand along the creek. At 3.0 miles, you'll enter a small canyon where the stream you've been following joins the main stream running from the left down Riprap Hollow. Just after the confluence, a small waterfall drops a few feet in the streambed.

At 3.1 miles, the Riprap Trail turns up to the right where an abandoned section of trail stays along the creek. The trail then swings back down to the creek and picks up the original trail. As you continue to descend Riprap Hollow, notice the Catawba rhododendron that bloom rose-purple in late May and June.

Ford the stream at 3.3 miles to continue down the left side, and soon after, pass a cascade splashing into a green pool. The trail then fords back across the stream. Continue straight down the rocky shore that was once an old roadway along the stream. You'll reach a junction at 4.0 miles. (The Wildcat Ridge Trail, hike 74, is to the left; the Riprap and Wildcat Ridge Trails, along with the AT, make a good loop hike of 9.3 miles.) Continue straight ahead.

The Riprap Trail goes down along the stream, emerging from the park at 4.9 miles and connecting with a fire road (it leads left in another mile to VA 612, which is out of the community of Crimora to the west).

74 | WILDCAT RIDGE TRAIL

Distance: 2.7 miles one-way
Difficulty: Moderate
Elevation loss: 1,300 feet
Cautions: Stream crossings
Connections: AT, Riprap Trail

Attractions: South-facing portions of this trail have a profusion of mountain laurel that blooms in May and June. You'll pass small pools in the stream where you can dangle your feet on a hot summer day. This trail, combined with the Riprap Trail (hike 73) and the Appalachian Trail (AT), forms a good loop hike. Be aware that fires in 1998 and 1999 burned the undergrowth in this part of the South District.

Trailhead: Stop at the Wildcat Ridge parking area on the right side of Skyline Drive at Mile 92.1.

Description: The Wildcat Ridge Trail descends from the parking area to cross the AT at 0.1 mile. (To the left, the AT reaches Jarman Gap in 5.8 miles; to the right, the AT leads to Riprap parking area in 2.7 miles. The Riprap Trail, hike 73, Wildcat Ridge Trail, and the AT can be used for a loop hike of 9.3 miles.) Continue straight down the Wildcat Ridge Trail.

You'll dip through a sag at 0.4 mile and then continue down the ridge. The trail curves left at 1.1 miles as it descends across a south-facing slope. Switchback right in the descent.

Follow a small hollow down in a steep descent to rockhop a tributary stream of Riprap Hollow at 2.0 miles. On the other side, the trail turns left to follow the creek downstream along an old roadway. At 2.3 miles, the trail leaves the old roadway to the right and switchbacks down to another rockhop of the stream at 2.4 miles as you descend farther into Riprap Hollow. At 2.6 miles, ford the main stream in Riprap Hollow and ascend to a junction with the Riprap Trail at 2.7 miles.

(To the left, the Riprap Trail reaches the park boundary in 0.9 mile. To the right, the Riprap Trail, hike 73, leads 3.6 miles up to the AT, where you can turn south to reach the Riprap parking area in another 0.4 mile.)

75 | TURK MOUNTAIN TRAIL

Distance: 1.1 miles one-way
Difficulty: Moderate
Elevation gain: 300 feet
Cautions: Talus slopes
Connections: AT, Turk Branch Trail, Turk Gap Trail

Attractions: You'll have a good view north from the summit of Turk Mountain, 2,981 feet.

Trailhead: Parking is on the left in Turk Gap at Mile 94.1; the Appalachian Trail (AT) crosses the drive in the gap. Walk across the drive to pick up the AT on the west, headed south. (The Turk Gap Trail, off to the right, follows an old road down the mountain to the park boundary in 1.7 miles, where there is no public access. On the east side of the drive, the AT heads north to Wildcat Ridge parking area in 2.2 miles. Also on the east, the Turk Branch Trail to the right follows an old road down the mountain 2.5 miles to connect with the South Fork of the Moormans River Fire Road.)

Description: Follow the AT down to the left. You'll pass through pine and laurel to reach a junction at 0.1 mile (the AT continues straight toward Jarman Gap in 3.5 miles); turn right on the Turk Mountain Trail.

The trail drops through a saddle, passes over a rise, and then begins an ascent of Turk Mountain at 0.4 mile. You'll cross talus slopes and then switchback right and left up through rocks at 0.9 mile. The trail reaches the ridgeline and turns to the right up to the rocky summit of Turk Mountain at 1.1 miles. Keep going up through the rocks to get to a great view north and west.

SELECTED REFERENCES

Conners, John A. *Shenandoah National Park, An Interpretive Guide.*
Blacksburg, Va.: The McDonald & Woodward Publishing Company,
1988.

Floyd, Tom. *Lost Trails and Forgotten People, The Story of Jones Mountain.*
Vienna, Va.: The Potomac Appalachian Trail Club, 1981.

Gathright II, Thomas M. *Geology of the Shenandoah National Park, Virginia.*
Charlottesville: Virginia Division of Mineral Resources, 1976.

Gupton, Oscar W., and Fred C. Swope. *Trees and Shrubs of Virginia.*
Charlottesville: University Press of Virginia, 1981.

————. *Wildflowers of the Shenandoah Valley and Blue Ridge Mountains.*
Charlottesville: University Press of Virginia, 1979.

Heatwole, Henry. *Guide to Shenandoah National Park and Skyline Drive.*
Luray, Va.: Shenandoah Natural History Association, 1978, updated
1990.

Lambert, Darwin. *Herbert Hoover's Hideaway.* Luray, Va.: Shenandoah
Natural History Association, 1971.

————. *The Undying Past of Shenandoah National Park.* Boulder, Co.:
Roberts Rinehart, Inc. Publishers, 1989.

Mazzeo, Peter M. *Trees of Shenandoah National Park.* Luray, Va.:
Shenandoah Natural History Association, 1986.

Pollock, George Freeman. *Skyland: The Heart of the Shenandoah National
Park.* Chesapeake Book Company, 1960.

Reeder, Carolyn, and Jack Reeder. *Shenandoah Heritage: The Story of the
People Before the Park.* Vienna, Va.: The Potomac Appalachian Trail
Club, 1978.

————. *Shenandoah Secrets: The Story of the Park's Hidden Past.* Vienna, Va.:
The Potomac Appalachian Trail Club, 1991.

————. *Shenandoah Vestiges: What the Mountain People Left Behind.* Vienna,
Va.: The Potomac Appalachian Trail Club, 1980.

Stanley, Steven M. *Earth and Life Through Time.* New York: W. H. Freeman
and Company, 1986.

Stoneberger, John W. *Memories of a Lewis Mountain Man.* Vienna, Va.: The
Potomac Appalachian Trail Club, 1993.

APPENDIX: RECOMMENDED RESOURCES

Appalachian Trail Conference
P.O. Box 807
Harpers Ferry, WV 25425-0807
888-287-8673

ARAMARK Shenandoah National Park Lodges
P.O. Box 727
Luray, VA 22835
800-999-4714
www.visitshenandoah.com

Potomac Appalachian Trail Club
118 Park Street SE
Vienna, VA 22180-4609
703-242-0693
www.patc.net

Shenandoah National Park
3655 US Hwy. 211E
Luray, VA 22835
540-999-3500
www.nps.gov/shen

Shenandoah National Park camping reservations
800-365-CAMP
http://reservations.nps.gov

Shenandoah Natural History Association
3655 US Hwy. 211E
Luray, VA 22835
540-999-3582
www.nps.gov/shen/snha/snhahome.htm

Trails Illustrated
National Geographic Maps
P.O. Box 4357
Evergreen, CO 80437-4357
www.trailsillustrated.com

INDEX

ABOUT THE AUTHOR

Russ Manning began his career as a science writer, but for the past ten years has devoted his attention to travel and outdoor subjects. He has authored several books about the Southeast, including *100 Hikes in the Great Smoky Mountains National Park, Exploring the Big South Fork: A Handbook to the National River and Recreation Area, 100 Trails of the Big South Fork: Tennessee and Kentucky,* and *40 Hikes in Tennessee's South Cumberland.* He has also written over 200 articles for such magazines as *Outside, Backpacker, The Tennessee Conservationist, Appalachia,* and *Environmental Ethics.*

THE MOUNTAINEERS, founded in 1906, is a nonprofit outdoor activity and conservation club, whose mission is "to explore, study, preserve, and enjoy the natural beauty of the outdoors. . . . " Based in Seattle, Washington, the club is now the third-largest such organization in the United States, with 15,000 members and five branches throughout Washington State.

The Mountaineers sponsors both classes and year-round outdoor activities in the Pacific Northwest, which include hiking, mountain climbing, ski-touring, snowshoeing, bicycling, camping, kayaking and canoeing, nature study, sailing, and adventure travel. The club's conservation division supports environmental causes through educational activities, sponsoring legislation, and presenting informational programs. All club activities are led by skilled, experienced volunteers, who are dedicated to promoting safe and responsible enjoyment and preservation of the outdoors.

If you would like to participate in these organized outdoor activities or the club's programs, consider a membership in The Mountaineers. For information and an application, write or call The Mountaineers, Club Headquarters, 300 Third Avenue West, Seattle, Washington 98119; (206) 284-6310.

The Mountaineers Books, an active, nonprofit publishing program of the club, produces guidebooks, instructional texts, historical works, natural history guides, and works on environmental conservation. All books produced by The Mountaineers are aimed at fulfilling the club's mission.

Send or call for our catalog of more than 300 outdoor titles:

The Mountaineers Books
1001 SW Klickitat Way, Suite 201
Seattle, WA 98134
800-553-4453
mbooks@mountaineers.org
www.mountaineersbooks.org

Other titles you may enjoy from The Mountaineers Books:

100 HIKES IN™ SERIES: These are our fully detailed, best-selling hiking guides with complete descriptions, maps, and photos. Chock-full of trail data, safety tips, and wilderness etiquette.

100 HIKES IN THE GREAT SMOKY MOUNTAINS NATIONAL PARK, 2nd Edition, Russ Manning

40 HIKES IN TENNESSEE'S SOUTH CUMBERLAND, 3rd Edition, Russ Manning

BACKPACKER'S EVERYDAY WISDOM: 1001 Expert Tips for Hikers, Karen Berger
Expert tips and tricks for hikers and backpackers selected from one of the most popular BACKPACKER magazine columns. Problem-solving techniques and brilliant improvisations show hikers how to make their way and make do in the backcountry.

ANIMAL TRACKS OF THE SOUTHEAST: Book and poster, Chris Stall
Contains information on more than 40 animals common to this region. This pocket-size guide contains life-size drawings of footprints and information on size, sounds, habitat, diet, and patterns of movement.

BACKPACKER'S WILDERNESS 911: A Step-by-Step Guide for Medical Emergencies and Improvised Care in the Backcountry, Eric A. Weiss, M.D.
Written by BACKPACKER medical editor and emergency room veteran, this guide covers the injuries and incidents most likely to happen in the backcountry. Instructions for self-care are kept simple and easy to follow.

WILDERNESS NAVIGATION: Finding Your Way Using Map, Compass, Altimeter & GPS, Bob Burns and Mike Burns
Backed by more than 60 years of field research, this book includes the most reliable and easy-to-learn methods of navigation yet devised.

CONDITIONING FOR OUTDOOR FITNESS, David Musnick, M.D, and Mark Pierce, A.T.C., with the assistance of Sandra K. Elliot, P.T.
Written by a team of sports fitness experts, this guide teaches key aerobic and strength-training concepts to meet the demands of your outdoor activities.

GPS MADE EASY: Using Global Positioning Systems in the Outdoors, 2nd Edition, Lawrence Letham
Up-to-date version of the handbook for understanding how GPS works. A practical guide for those who ski, climb, or hike above the treeline, and also helpful for sea kayakers or those who work in remote, featureless areas.